Only Have Eyes for You
Exploring Canine Research with The Science Dog

Linda P. Case

Only Have Eyes for You
Exploring Canine Research with The Science Dog
Linda P. Case

AutumnGold Publishing
A Division of AutumnGold Consulting
Mahomet, IL 61853
www.autumngoldconsulting.com

ISBN-13: 978-1508862086
ISBN-10: 1508862087

Other Books by Linda P. Case

Beware the Straw Man: The Science Dog Explores Dog
Training Fact & Fiction

Dog Food Logic: Making Smart Decisions for your Dog
in an Age of Too Many Choices

Canine and Feline Nutrition: A Resource for Companion
Animal Professionals

The Dog: Its Behavior, Nutrition and Health

The Cat: Its Behavior, Nutrition and Health

Canine and Feline Behavior and Training: A Complete
Guide to Understanding our Two Best Friends

For
Cooper, Chip, Vinnie
and the wee one, Alice

Table of Contents

Introduction

We live in an exciting time for dogs and dog people. By "dog people" I mean those (and there seem to be a lot of us) who live with one or more dogs (usually more), love dogs, enjoy reading about and learning more about dogs, participate in one or more dog activities and perhaps, if you are really lucky, get to work in a dog-related profession. The reason that we live in exciting times is that for the last 15 years, the study of the domestic dog has exploded. Throughout the world, scientists from a wide range of disciplines are interested in the dog's evolutionary history, genetics, cognitive abilities, social behavior, response to various types of training, nutritional needs, health, and longevity. Most of these studies are taking place in academia, in large part at universities that house "dog labs", a new breed of research facility that invites dogs and their owners from surrounding communities and in some cases (for on-line studies) from around the world, to participate in their studies. Similarly, some (but certainly not all) nutrition and feeding studies take place in academic settings while others are conducted in the private sector by pet food companies. Although the inclusion of pet dogs who live in homes is less common in nutrition studies, it is becoming increasingly so as researchers reach out to include "citizen scientist" dog owners in their research (see *Scoopin' for Science* in Part 1 for an example).

Collectively, this new phenomenon of dog science is producing massive volumes of research papers that are published in a variety of different academic journals. These journals are distributed to (and unfortunately are often available exclusively to)......other scientists. Although the information that is provided by these papers is of great interest to the many dog folks and professionals who train, care for and love dogs, it is often not available to those outside of academic communities. This book, like *"Beware the Straw Man"* before it, attempts to bridge that gap by bringing the results of new and exciting dog research to members of the dog world. *"Only Have Eyes for You"* contains a set of 32 essays summarizing more than 50 new research papers that cover topics that are near and dear to the hearts of all dog people. The essays focus on three primary areas of canine study – nutrition and feeding (*Part 1 - What's for Dinner*), training and cognition (*Part 2 – Smarty Pants*), and controversial topics that are frequently debated by dog owners or that impact the relationships that we have with dogs (*Part 3 – Stirring Things Up*).

Part 1, *What's for Dinner*, takes a look at pet food ingredients, food quality, and issues associated with the regulation and marketing of commercial pet foods. The first three essays review studies of pet food labeling infractions and the potential impacts that these may have on pet health and consumer (pet owner) trust. The first of the essays, *"What's in Your Food?"* reviews a series of four studies finding that a substantial proportion of dog foods are mislabeled – they either contain protein ingredients that are not reported on the label or completely lack one or more of the ingredients that are reported on the product label. This research is followed up by a laudable project conducted in the UK in which the researchers (unlike their predecessors) reveal the brand names and the manufacturers of the pet foods that they studied, some of which had multiple labeling violations (*"What's in Your Food – Naming Names"*). Finally, *"What's in Your (Vegetarian) Food?"* applies the same analytical techniques to pet foods that are labeled and sold as "vegetarian" (spoiler alert – the news is not good).

Part 1 then shifts focus to examine several dog food issues that are of current concern to dog owners. At the top of the list is the controversy regarding the difference between meals and by-product meals. For the facts regarding the production and quality of these ingredients, see *"What's the Deal with Meals?"*. The measurement of dog food quality is further explored in *"Scoopin' for Science"* and *"How Reactive is Your Lysine"*, while the nutritional value and safety of popular dog chews and treats are critically reviewed in *"Keep Those Doggies Rollin....Rawhide, Rawhide!"* and *"Got Gullet?"*.

We then tackle a rather sensitive topic – the documented epidemic of obesity in pet dogs. Two essays examine why it is that owners (and some veterinarians) fail to recognize overweight conditions in dogs. The third piece, somewhat humorously, examines an unusual approach to weight reduction that a major pet food company has studied (*"Air – It's What's for Dinner"*). The section closes with two chapters that examine the current state of pet food marketing and how current advertising trends may be influencing our dog food selections. (*"The Nature of Natural"* and *"Pet Food Marketing – Science Weighs In"*).

Part 2, *Smarty Pants* is devoted to those dog folks who, like me, are fascinated by new information regarding canine cognition, behavior and training. If you are interested in learning more about the dog's social behavior and how dogs naturally communicate with people, take a look at the first group of essays in this section. The first, which carries the title of this book, examines how dogs may use human gaze to learn things about their environment and how different factors in a dog's life might interfere with those abilities. Other essays examine factors that influence a dog's inclination to seek help from his or her owner (*"With a Little Help from My Friends"*), whether dogs are capable of taking the perspective of others (*"Do You Know What I Can See?"*), and how skilled dogs are at observational learning (*"Doggie See, Doggie Do"*).

A variety of different training philosophies and techniques are also the subject of research today. Remote training devices are used by many trainers for a variety of purposes. I recently trained our youngest dog, Ally, to stay on a pause table using a popular remote trainer. My experiences and a pair of research studies that examined the effectiveness of these devices are reported in *"Manners Minder and Me"*. If you have read any of my earlier books, including *"Beware the Straw Man"* you will know that I am a dedicated clicker trainer and advocate for both clicker training and training techniques that emphasize the use of positive reinforcement. The next three essays, beginning with *"The Meaning of Click"* examine how the "click" may actually work with dogs, how dogs respond to different types of cues, and factors that influence how effectively dogs learn in a training class environment. The final essays in this section are devoted to canine communication and emotions. Anyone who lives with and loves dogs will enjoy learning more about play bows (*"I Bow for Your Play"*), expressions of empathy and concern between dogs (*"I Feel Your Pain"*), and how dogs are capable of developing friendships not only with other dogs, but with members of other species (*"My Best Friend's Friends"*). I hope that you enjoy reading these essays as much as I enjoyed writing them.

The final section of the book contains a diverse set of essays whose primary central theme is that they tackle topics that are either hot subjects of debate among dog trainers and behaviorists (*"Death Throes of the Guilty Look"* and "*How Many Barks Does a Nuisance Dog Make?"*) or are somewhat controversial among different groups of dog owners and professionals (*"Pretty in Pink"*, "*A Walk in the Park"* and *"Excitable You"*). To finish out the book, the final two essays take a look at human perceptions of dogs, first by asking (humorously at times) people to report what they believe to be attributes of their perfect dog. The final essay examines some of the *actual* canine attributes that tend to attract our attentions and our love (*"Go Ask Alice"*). Whatever type of dog person you may be, this section should have a chapter that interests you and provokes thought.

As in *"Beware the Straw Man"* this book focuses on presenting recently acquired scientific evidence that applies directly to the care and training of our dogs. However, it is inevitable that as a canine nutritionist and trainer, I have personal opinions about these topics. To alert the reader to those instances when I am straying from the dominion of science into the realm of opinion, the book includes this always charming icon:

Up on my Soapbox

You are welcome to read my opinions, to agree or not agree, and to find additional evidence in support or in dissent of the presented science. Like *"Beware the Straw Man"* the ultimate goal of *"Only Have Eyes for You"* is to encourage all who love dogs to seek out the scientific evidence that supports or fails to support your beliefs, to read with your critical thinking skills in full gear, and to make informed and defendable decisions regarding the foods that you select for your dog, the training techniques that you use, and the decisions that you make for your dog's social well-being and emotional health. Once you accomplish this, you are more than welcome to join me (or not) up on the soap box!

Part 1 – What's for Dinner?

1
What's in YOUR Food?

What I mean of course, is "What's in your dog's food?"

When asked this question, most owners read the list of ingredients found on the pet food label. By law, pet food ingredients must be reported in descending order of preponderance by weight at the time of processing. This means that ingredients that are found first in the list are present in greatest abundance in the food.

There are several limitations regarding the type of information that the pet food ingredient list provides to consumers, and I discuss these in detail in *Dog Food Logic*. However, until recently, it was generally presumed that misrepresenting food ingredients, for example listing an ingredient that is not actually present in the food or failing to identify others, was *not* one of those limitations. Unfortunately, it appears that such a presumption may be ill-founded.

Several research studies published in the scientific literature over the past four years have shown that at least some brands of commercial dog food have ingredient lists that do not always conform to what is actually *in* the food.

Study 1: Four brands of dry dog food that are marketed as novel protein source diets containing venison were tested for the presence of other protein sources (1). Of the four products, two listed chicken and one listed rice protein in addition to venison on their label ingredient panel. ***Results:*** Of the four foods, three tested positive for the presence of soy protein and one tested positive for the presence of beef protein. In all of these cases, neither beef nor soy products were reported in the product's ingredient list. (It is interesting and somewhat ironic to note that one of the foods that tested positive for soy protein carried a front label claim stating "*No Soy!*").

Study 2: The same team of researchers tested four retail dry dog foods that carried a "No Soy" label claim and seven therapeutic dry foods marketed to veterinarians for use in diagnosing soy allergies in dogs (2). ***Results:*** Soy protein was detected in three of the four retail brands. Of the seven veterinary-prescribed foods, four were found to contain low levels of soy protein.

Study 3: Eleven limited ingredient diets (LIDs) and one veterinary-prescribed hydrolyzed protein product were tested for the presence of animal origin ingredients not reported on their ingredient label (3). This study used DNA analysis and microscopic analysis of food particles that allowed the distinction between mammal, fish, and bird tissues. ***Results:*** Of the 12 products, the species of animal identified by microscopic and DNA analysis matched the food label's ingredient list *in only two*. In the remaining 10 products, bone tissue fragments from one or more unreported animal source proteins were present.

Study 4: Finally, a comprehensive study published in the journal *Food Control* examined the content of 52 brands of commercial dog and cat food using DNA analysis. ***Results:*** Of the 52 products, 31 (60 %) had no labeling violations, meaning that the protein ingredients that were reported in the ingredient list completely matched the sources that were identified via DNA analysis. However, 21 brands (40 %) contained protein sources that were not listed on the ingredient list or, in one case, a protein source that could not be identified. *In three of these products, the protein source listed on the ingredient panel was entirely absent from the food.* Chicken was the most commonly undeclared protein source in the mislabeled foods. This is not surprising because chicken is generally the least expensive source of animal protein in pet foods. Mislabeling was also more frequently observed in canned (wet) pet foods than in dry pet foods. The presence of goat meat (yes, you read that correctly) was found in 9 products.

Seven of these identified another animal species source such as chicken or beef on their label and did *not* include the more generic "meat" term nor (obviously) "goat meat" as an ingredient.

Take Away for Dog Folks: The authors of the first three papers wrote that their objectives were to examine LIDs for the presence of undeclared protein ingredients. Their concern was the increased use of these foods by owners and some veterinarians to diagnose food-related allergies in dogs. If you are not familiar with it, the standard diagnostic approach when food allergy is suspected is to feed a food that contains a single and novel (or hydrolyzed) protein source to the dog for 8 to 10 weeks. This is called an elimination diet and its purpose is to prevent exposure to all potential food allergens. If a dog's signs diminish, the elimination diet trial is considered positive for adverse food reaction (food allergy) and an attempt is made to identify protein sources that the dog can tolerate. The scientists' concern was that owners were unwittingly using the LIDs as an alternative to the more expensive and supposedly better controlled veterinary-prescribed foods. The expectation was that the therapeutic foods would contain only what their labels claimed, while the retail LIDs would be contaminated with other ingredients. What they found however, was that *both* retail foods and veterinary-prescribed foods have the potential to be mislabeled. (*Oops*).

Regardless of results not always showing what one expects, there are several important issues that these studies expose:

1. **Intentional or accidental?** The analytical tests used in these studies are able to detect very small quantities of undeclared protein sources. Therefore, a positive result does not necessarily mean that the source was contributing a large proportion of the food's protein. It only means that an undeclared protein source was present. This might occur accidentally as a result of ingredient cross-contamination during transportation, via airborne particle transfer in the manufacturing plant, or through the use of equipment that was not thor-

oughly cleaned between production runs. Regardless of intent, these causes are still problems and should be addressed in good manufacturing practice and quality control procedures. Alternatively, the identification of chicken as the most frequently undeclared animal protein source certainly suggests the potential for intentional substitution and mislabeling, seeing that chicken is less expensive than the ingredients that it augmented or replaced. Because these studies did not investigate the quantities of undeclared ingredients nor whether or not their presence was intentional, these are questions that still need to be answered.

2. **Diagnosing/managing allergic dogs:** For those who live with dogs suspected of having a food allergy, these results are bad news regardless of knowing quantities or intent. Although the concentration of a food allergen that is needed to trigger an allergic response in dogs is not known, it is expected to be similar to that in people - very low. These studies suggest that feeding a veterinary-prescribed elimination diet is not a guarantee that the dog will not be exposed to a suspected allergen such as soy. In addition, feeding a dog a retail brand LID may not be an effective approach even when food allergens have been identified. For these reasons, some veterinarians and nutritionists recommend feeding a homemade elimination diet for the diagnosis of food allergies in dogs. Once the allergenic protein is identified, extreme care will be needed during food selection.

3. **Trust:** Last, but certainly not least, are the issues of food mislabeling, manufacturing integrity and consumer trust. The cases reported in the most recent study, in which listed ingredients were completely absent from some foods and were substituted with other protein ingredients, are in clear violation of AAFCO labeling regulations. The researchers of that study had purchased the sample foods from retail vendors, which indicates that these violations are occurring without detection. What is not known is whether ingredient substitu-

tions, additions, and mislabeling are intentional or accidental or where within the production chain these adulterations are taking place. What does seem clear however, is that consumers cannot always trust the ingredient list to represent only and all ingredients that are present in the food.

What is a dog person to do?? Remember that a substantial proportion of products that were tested in these studies contained all and only those protein ingredients that their labels reported. They were *not* mislabeled. If you feed commercial dog food, seek out reputable manufacturers. These are the producers who provide ingredient source information, manufacturing details, safety records, and detailed product information to their consumers. Moreover, ask questions, request information, demand transparency and be a critical thinker (and consumer) for your dog so that you have a better chance of *knowing* what is in YOUR (dog's) food.

Cited Studies:

1. Raditic DM, Remillard RL, Tater KC. ELISA testing for common food antigens in four dry dog foods used in dietary elimination trials. *Journal of Animal Physiology and Animal Nutrition* 2010; 95:90-97.

2. Willis-Mahn C, Remillard R, Tater K. ELISA testing for soy antigens in dry dog foods used in dietary elimination trials. *Journal of the American Animal Hospital Association* 2014; 50:383-389.

3. Ricci R, Granato A, Vascellari M, Boscarato M, Palagiano C, Andrighetto I, Diez M, Mutinelli F. Identification of undeclared sources of animal origin in canine dry foods used in dietary elimination trials. *Journal of Animal Physiology and Animal Nutrition* 2013; 97:32-38.

4. Okuma TA, Hellberg RS. Identification of meat species in pet foods using a real-time polymerase chain reaction (PCR) assay. *Food Control* 2015; 50:9-17.

2
What's in Your Food – Naming Names

The previous studies of pet food mislabeling withheld the brand names of the foods that they studied. In this study, the researchers decided to start naming names.

In the previous essay, "*What's in Your Food?*" I reviewed the results of four published studies that compared the animal protein ingredients listed on various pet food labels with the *actual* ingredients found in the foods. (It probably came as a surprise to some that those two entities are not always the same). Those studies found multiple instances of mislabeling in which undeclared animal species protein sources were included as ingredients and/or protein ingredients that were declared on the label were completely absent.

Another study was published recently (1). Although this work was conducted in the UK and examined canned pet foods only, it was unique in one important way. Unlike the four previous studies, this group of researchers revealed the brand names of every single product that they examined.

All I can say is; it's about time.

The Study: According to the authors, the objective of their study was to "*examine the correlation between the composition of different animal proteins and the animal species disclosed on pet food labels*". Now, a naïve person might assume that such a correlation would be, oh, in the vicinity of, say.....**1.0**. But, we now know that this is not only naïve, but an assumption that has already been shown to be patently false.

In the present study, the authors tested 17 different brands of canned (i.e. wet) dog or cat foods available for purchase at UK supermarkets for the presence of cow, chicken, pig and horse meat DNA.

Results: None of the foods contained horsemeat. However, there the good news ends. Of the 17 foods, animal species that were *not* listed on the food's label were found in 14 (**82 %**) of the products. Several discrepancies that are worth noting include:

- Hill's Prescription Diet R/D Feline Weight Loss listed chicken immediately after pork on its ingredient panel, yet contained **no chicken** (0 percent).

- Seven products included the phrase "*with beef*" in their brand name or prominently displayed on the label. The protein in four of these foods came predominantly from pork and chicken (75 to 86 % of protein). These products included a Pedigree (Mars) brand, two Nestle'-Purina brands, and a UK private label brand.

- A Mars brand (Chappie) that stated "*14 % whitefish*" on its ingredient panel actually contained **no fish at all**; 100% of its protein came from chicken. An ALDI private label brand called "*Salmon in Pate*" listed fish first on its label, did not report chicken at all, and yet was 92 % chicken.

- Of six pet foods that highlighted "*chicken*" on the label or in their brand name, two products, both private label brands, contained more pig or beef protein than chicken protein.

Up on my Soapbox

Up on the Box: The authors of this study note that technically most (not all) of these foods were still in compliance with EU pet food regulations. The finding of large proportions of chicken and pork in foods that reported no such species on their ingredient panels was still in compliance provided the term "*meat and animal derivatives*" was found somewhere on the ingredient list. Unbeknownst to most consumers, this term includes "*all products and derivatives of the processing......of warm-blooded land animals*". This covers everything from chickens to well, pretty much anything that has blood and feet. The EU regulations cast a pretty wide net for their pet food manufacturers.

The second issue is the ubiquitous word "*with*". Similar to regulations in the United States, EU standards require that pet foods using this descriptor contain....wait for it.....a minimum of only 4% of the designated ingredient. (In the US, the minimum is a whopping 3 %). And as these products demonstrate, 4 percent is about what you get.

As the authors of this study note, and I agree, there appears to be a serious mismatch between label standards in the pet food industry and what consumers are led to believe about the foods that they purchase for their animal companions. Is it not reasonable for my friend Alice to expect that the food she selects for her Yorkie called "*Gourmet Terrine with Chicken and Game*" actually contain more than 1 percent of its protein from chicken, not as is the reality, almost 90 percent of it coming from beef? And when my elderly neighbor Joe carefully selects food for his beloved cat Pumpkin, is it silly for him to expect that "*Felix Complete with Beef*" contains a substantial proportion of, say......beef?

Just as we need increased transparency from the pet food (and human food) industry regarding the source of ingredients, processing methods, measures of quality, and safety records, it appears that we also need regulations that prevent rather than support misleading label claims and brand names. Is it really too much to ask that a pet food actually contains what it claims to contain (and nothing else)?

Cited Study: Maine IR, Atterbury R, Chang KC. Investigation into the animal species contents of popular wet pet foods. *Acta Veterinaria Scandinavica* 2015; 57:7-11.

3
What's in Your (Vegetarian) Food?

Regardless of your views about feeding vegetarian foods to dogs, I think that we can all agree that a food that is labeled "vegetarian" should actually BE vegetarian.

Here we go again.

It appears that there may be more than what dog owners expect to find in vegetarian dog food.

Hold the Spam, Please: Before all of the *"Dogs are Carnivores (and a pox on your mother if you think differently)"* devotees begin sputtering that dogs should not be fed a vegetarian diet in the first place, let me state that this is *not* what this essay is about. So please, don't even start. The point of this essay is not to argue (*again.....*) whether or not dogs have an absolute requirement for meat in their diet (here's a hint: They don't). Rather, in this piece I examine new information about undeclared ingredients that may be present in dog food and the mounting evidence of regulatory violations within the pet food industry.

In this newest pair of studies, a team of veterinary nutritionists at the University of California tested vegetarian pet foods for label compliance and ingredient content. Unfortunately once again, the news isn't good.

Label Compliance: In the first study, the researchers collected samples of 24 dog and cat food brands that carried a label claim of "vegetarian" (1). The majority of the foods were over-the-counter products purchased at a local pet supply store. Three products were veterinary therapeutic diets. Of the group of products, 19 were formulated for dogs or for dogs and cats, and five were formulated exclusively for cats. Product labels were examined for their compliance with the Association of American Feed Control Official (AAFCO) model regulations, which are the basis for most state mandated pet food regulations. Pet food samples were also analyzed for total protein and essential amino acid content.

Results: Of the 24 foods, only eight (33%) were in complete compliance with AAFCO label regulations. This means that 16 brands (66%) had one or more violations. The most common infractions were the omission of feeding instructions or caloric content, improperly reported guaranteed analysis panels, and mislabeled ingredient statements. Nutrient analysis showed that all but one of the foods met AAFCO's minimum crude protein requirements. However, six brands had deficient levels of one or more of the essential amino acids. This means that while the total amount of protein that the food contained appeared to be sufficient, essential amino acid requirements, which are more important, were not always met.

Presence of animal-based ingredients: In a second study, the same group of researchers tested 14 brands of vegetarian pet foods (2). They purchased each food on two occasions to obtain samples as duplicates from different manufacturing batches. Six were dry and eight were canned products. Samples were analyzed for the presence of mammalian DNA using an accepted laboratory technique called multiplex polymerase chain reaction (PCR). Since all 24 foods were marketed as vegetarian (and in some cases, as vegan), none included animal-based components in their list of ingredients.

Results: All six of the dry (extruded) foods that were tested contained DNA from beef, pork or sheep and five of the six contained DNA from multiple animal species. These results were consistent across batches for all 7 products. Only one of the 8 canned vegetarian foods contained animal DNA (beef) and this finding was not repeated in the second sample. In this study, the researchers also tested for the DNA of dogs, cats, goats, deer, horses, rats, mice and rabbits. DNA from these species was not detected in any of the samples. Similar to earlier studies that have found the DNA of undeclared meats in dog foods, the amount of animal-based ingredients in the foods could not be quantified. The researchers could not speculate whether the labeling violations were a result of deliberate adulteration or unintentional cross-contamination of vegetarian products with meat-containing foods produced at the same facility.

Up on my Soapbox

Soap Box Time: The Federal Food, Drug and Cosmetic Act requires that all pet foods sold in the United States are safe, produced under sanitary conditions, contain no harmful substances, and ***are truthfully labeled*** (emphasis mine). Perhaps I am being picky, but labeling a food as vegetarian and then not ensuring that the food indeed *lacks* the meat of cows, pigs and sheep, seems to qualify as not being truthful. (Some might even call it lying, I suppose). Not only are such egregious errors in violation of both FDA and AAFCO regulations, but they seriously impact the trust that dog owners have in pet food manufacturers. And rightly so.

To date, the majority of pet owners in the US continue to feed dry, extruded food. Of the dry-type vegetarian foods tested in this study, *all of them, 100 %* were, in fact, not vegetarian at all. This leads one to ponder about other products on the market and whether it is more the norm than the exception for dry dog foods that are sold as vegetarian to be nothing of the sort. While the authors note that this was a small number of products and so do not represent all vegetarian foods, the fact that all of the foods failed their DNA tests is alarming.

What can you do as a dog owner? Contact the manufacturer of your food and ask them how they verify the integrity of their products, specifically, the ingredients that they include in their foods. If they are not forthcoming and transparent with their response, find a producer who is. The good news is that the pressure that research studies such as these place on pet food companies and upon the industry as a whole will hopefully encourage increased transparency and improved regulatory oversight - something that we are apparently in dire need of.

Cited Studies:

1. Kanakubo K, Fascetti AJ, Larsen JA. Assessment of protein and amino acid concentrations and labeling adequacy of commercial vegetarian diets formulated for dogs and cats. *Journal of the American Veterinary Medical Association* 2015; 247:385-392.
2. Kanakubo, K, Fascetti AJ, Larsen JA. Determination of mammalian deoxyribonucleic acid (DNA) in commercial vegetarian and vegan diets for dogs and cats. *Animal Physiology and Animal Nutrition* 2016; doi: 10.1111/jpn.12506.

4
What's the Deal with Meals?

Does it matter whether your dog food contains chicken meal versus chicken by-product meal?

In early May of 2014, Nestle'-Purina, the largest producer of pet foods sold in the US, filed a lawsuit against Blue Buffalo, a competitor company. The lawsuit alleged that Blue Buffalo's marketing claims that their foods contained no by-product meals were false and disparaging to other companies' products. According to the report of a testing laboratory that had been hired by Purina, at least some Blue Buffalo brands did indeed contain poultry by-product meal, comprising up to 25 percent of the meal in some of Blue Buffalo's products. As is the way of the pet food industry, Blue Buffalo responded within days with a counter-suit of their own, accusing Purina of defamation, unfair competition, and false advertising.

Central to this public (dog) food fight was the belief, strongly promoted by Blue Buffalo, that chicken or poultry *meals* are of superior nutritional value to *by-product meals* and that high quality dog foods contain meals and reject the use of by-product meals. (It is of interest to note that Purina cleverly side-steps the nutrient quality issue in their lawsuit. Rather they contest that Blue Buffalo has falsely promoted itself as being completely transparent to its customers).

Initially, Blue Buffalo responded to Nestlé's allegations with denial. Both companies launched public campaigns that included strongly worded letters to their pet parents (i.e. consumers). However, in October of the same year, Blue Buffalo was made to eat crow (meal?) when they announced that one of their ingredient suppliers, Texas-based Wilbur-Ellis, had mislabeled an ingredient, which resulted in the presence of poultry by-product meal in some of their foods. In the words of Blue Buffalo's founder Bill Bishop: "*So while their [Wilbur-Ellis's] customers were ordering and paying for 100 percent chicken meal, at times they were receiving shipments that contained poultry by-product meal. As a result, we have stopped doing business with this plant.*"

So what is the truth? Are by-product meals lower in quality when compared with meals? Should discerning dog owners avoid chicken or poultry by-product meal and choose only foods that contain chicken or poultry meal? Is this the best way to distinguish between high quality dog foods and foods of lesser quality? Perhaps the best place to start is with an understanding of what a *meal* is in the first place.

Meals – The Protein Ingredient: Every ingredient that goes into a dog food contains a unique set of essential nutrients that it contributes to the finished product. In commercially prepared dry (extruded) dog foods, two primary types of meals are used to provide dietary protein:

1. ***Plant-source protein meals:*** Examples of commonly used plant-based protein meals are corn gluten meal, soybean meal and pea protein (or meal). In general, plant-based protein sources are an inexpensive source of protein and are found in foods that are marketed to pet owners interested in economy. The quality of these meals is moderate to low in terms of amino acid balance and digestibility, although several protein sources are used to ensure that all essential amino acid needs are met.

2. ***Animal-source protein meals:*** These meals vary tremendously in both source (species of animals) and in quality measures such as digestibility, amino acid content, and amino acid availability. Examples of species-specific meals that are commonly used in pet foods are chicken, bison, beef, salmon, venison, turkey and lamb meals. They meals may also be classified more largely as poultry meal (contains vary-

28

ing amounts of chicken, turkey or duck), fish meal (contains multiple fish species), or meat meal (contains varying amounts of pork, beef or sheep).

The Origins of Animal Meals: Animal-source meals are commercially produced through the process of *rendering*. Rendering is a cooking process that converts slaughterhouse products that have been deemed unfit for human consumption into a form that is regulated as acceptable for use in pet foods. These animal parts are those that are not typically consumed in our Western diet and include organ meats such as spleen, kidneys, liver, stomach and intestines, as well as varying amounts of bone and in the case of poultry animals, necks, feet, and heads. During the slaughter process, these parts are classified as "*inedible*", a designation that changes the supply stream into which the materials enter and that impacts the way in which they are handled, transported and processed. In addition to slaughterhouse waste, animals that end up at the rendering plant may also include "spent" layer chickens from the egg industry and food animals that were found to be diseased or injured and did not pass inspection for use as human foods.

During the rendering process, these combined components are ground, mixed and heated to a high temperature (220° to 270° F) that cooks the product, kill microbes and sterilizes the mixture. Sterilization is necessary because refrigeration is not required for the handling or transport of inedible foods. The resulting slurry is then centrifuged at a high speed to remove lipids (fat). The removed fat is further processed and eventually is sold separately as chicken fat, poultry fat, or animal fat. The mixture that remains is dried and ground to a uniform particle size that ultimately has the appearance and texture of dry corn meal. Animal protein meals are very low in moisture and contain between 55 and 65 percent protein, making them a rich source of protein when included in a pet food.

From a commercial perspective, meals are well suited for use in dry pet foods because they can be stored and transported easily and because they have a low moisture content that is necessary for extrusion processing. By comparison, high-moisture protein ingredients, such as "fresh" chicken (or other meat) only contribute small amounts of protein by weight to the end product because the water content is cooked off during extrusion. These ingredients may be listed first on a food's ingredient list simply because they contain more than 60 percent water and ingredients must be listed in predominance by weight at the time of processing. In reality, it is the dried meals, usually found within the first three to five ingredients on the list, that provide the bulk of dietary protein to dry dog foods.

Meals versus By-Product Meals: The protein meal designator that is receiving a lot of attention, as evidenced by Blue Buffalo's (and others') advertising campaigns, is the term *by-product*. It is important to know that you will see this term applied on pet food labels *only* to the meals of chicken and poultry. This distinction occurs because the Association of American Feed Control Officials (AAFCO) sets the definitions for ingredient terms and they have not designated a by-product meal term for any other animal protein ingredient. (The closest is meat meals versus meat and bone meals, in which the latter contains bone, which can reduce its quality as a protein source). So what exactly *is* the difference between chicken (poultry) meal and chicken (poultry) by-product meal?

According to AAFCO, the term *"meal"* refers to the *"dry, rendered product from a combination of clean flesh and skin with or without accompanying bone, derived from the parts of whole carcasses of [chicken/poultry], exclusive of feathers, heads, feet and entrails"*(1). Although this definition seems to suggest that meals are produced from the same parts of the chicken that make it to the supermarket for human consumption, this is not true. As discussed previously, animal protein meals are produced from slaughterhouse waste and other food animals that are deemed "not for human consumption" (i.e. inedible). In the case of chicken, this is the "chicken frame", the remaining portion of a chicken's body that remains after the meats destined for human consumption have been removed. More than 70 percent of a broiler chicken ends up in the supermarket, leaving about 30 percent in the frame, which is made up of a bit of muscle meat plus a lot of connective tissue and bone. In fact, no meals are produced from edible (human grade) meats because rendering plants are in the business of taking inedible animal parts and converting them into a form that can be fed to non-human animals.

Chicken (or poultry) *by-product* meal on the other hand is composed of the same chicken components that are included in meals, with the difference that by-product meals may *also* contain varying amounts of *chicken heads, chicken feet and chicken guts (viscera)*. Therefore, the difference between a chicken (or poultry) meal and its respective by-product meal is the inclusion of heads and necks, feet, and guts (viscera) in the latter and the exclusion of those body parts from the former. On the face of it, this appears to be an obvious quality distinction. After all, any product that has heads, feet and entrails in it not only sounds yucky, but certainly must also be of poor quality, right?

Well.....it depends.

Certainly the general (and understandable) perception is that, given this definition, meals will be of higher quality than by-product meals. This is clearly the conclusion that Blue Buffalo and other pet food companies that make *"No By-Products!"* claims on their labels are banking on. However, consistent and substantial quality differences between the two ingredient types are not reported. Rather, the inclusion of the additional body parts of heads, feet and guts in by-product meals can either reduce, maintain or improve the quality of a meal (2). The reason for this is that these three additional parts, although certainly not very appetizing to most humans, have varying nutritional value as food ingredients.

31

First, the protein quality of viscera (i.e. internal organs and intestinal contents) is similar to that of chicken flesh components that are included in very high quality chicken meals (and to what humans consume in a chicken dinner). In other words, including organ meats and intestinal contents in a by-product meal does not negatively affect the meal's protein quality and may even improve it in a poor or average quality meal. Second, the inclusion of (yuck) chicken heads to the mix results in a *slight* reduction in nutritional quality. This is because chicken *brains* are highly digestible while chicken *skulls*, being comprised of bone, are less so. So it appears to be a zero sum game when it comes to the added chicken heads. Last - chicken feet. As a food ingredient, feet are simply bad and have measured quality values similar to feeding connective tissue or bone residue.

Collectively, including varying amounts of the additional body parts (heads, feet or guts) in a by-product meal can affect the resultant product's protein quality either positively or negatively when compared with its corresponding meal. This depends somewhat upon the actual proportion of the three different body parts that are included in the end product, information by the way that a consumer is never privy to. If there are lots of guts, quality improves. Heads; could go either way. Feet; bad news.

Why All of the Hype? Studies of the digestibility and protein quality of meals and by-product meals have found that as a group meals are *slightly* more digestible and contain *slightly* more available essential amino acids than their associated by-product meals (3, 4). However, there is also a lot of overlap between the two ingredient groups, meaning that a given meal may be better, equal to or even lower in quality than a given by-product meal. Overall, the differences that have been found are neither dramatic nor worthy of the hysteria that seems to accompany the word *by-product* among dog owners and some pet food companies. Therefore, the marketing hyperbole and excessive "patting oneself on the back" by companies that include meals but not by-product meals should be viewed by all dog owners with a hefty dose of skepticism. True, there is some difference, but probably not enough of a quality difference to warrant all of the inflammatory language and excessive claims that are being made by companies that are jumping on the by-product free bandwagon. Ironically, consumers have no direct way to know if the meal that is used in the food that they select is of low, moderate or high quality, let alone the extent of the difference between a given meal and by-product meal. Moreover, there is no evidence showing one way or another if the measured and reported differences between chicken meals and chicken by-product meals have an effect upon dogs' overall nutritional health.

I would suggest that this exaggeration of difference has occurred (and has been actively promoted) because there are so few available ways for dog owners to accurately assess the quality of pet food ingredients in commercial pet foods. As a result, this single AAFCO-defined difference (meals vs. by-product meals) has caught on like a house on fire, with marketing campaigns flinging additional gasoline to fuel the flames and causing the distinction (one that really has little difference) to garner more importance than it warrants.

What We Can Know: It is an unfortunate paradox that one of the most important nutrients for dogs (protein) is supplied by a type of ingredient (protein meals) for which consumers are privy to very little information regarding source and quality. This is especially concerning given that animal-source meals can vary tremendously in the components that make them up and ultimately in their quality (i.e. in nutrient content and digestibility). What information *is* available to consumers to use (and what is hidden from us)? Sadly, there is much more of the latter than the former.

Animal-source proteins are generally better balanced in terms of amino acid content when compared with plant-based proteins and should be the preferred sources of protein in a quality diet. When assessing animal-source protein meals, choosing a meal from a named species is somewhat helpful. When you see a named species of animal, such as chicken, beef, salmon, bison, etc., as the major protein ingredient, this is generally indicative of a higher quality product (or at least a better regulated product). Ingredient supply companies are required to keep these ingredient streams separate and designated, which translates to a more uniform product and greater regulatory oversight. Conversely, the generic term used to describe a group of food animals (poultry, meat or fish meal), means that the meal may contain a mixture of species with no guarantee of any particular animal species or proportions in a given meal. At the production level this means that several ingredient streams are combined, with varying sources of origin, regulatory oversight, and quality attributes. Additionally, the species source that is least expensive in the marketplace at a given point in time may increase in proportion in its respective meal. Because of these differences, generic (combined) meals are less expensive to manufacturers than are species-specific meals.

What We Need to Know: These three designators: plant- vs. animal-source, species vs. generic group, and meal vs. by-product meal (for chicken/poultry) are the only protein ingredient quality designators that are available to dog owners via pet food labels. This might not be an issue if these were in truth the most important quality differences among animal protein meals. However, they are not. There are ways in which animal protein meals differ that are invisible to consumers and that can significantly influence the quality of the foods in which they are used.

Animal-source protein meals contain varying amounts of bone and connective tissues (this pertains to both meals and by-product meals), which affects both the protein quality and the mineral balance of the product. Bone matrix and connective tissues contain the protein collagen, which is poorly digested and utilized when included as a dietary protein source, while bone

34

contributes excess amounts of calcium and several other minerals. Meals that are high in collagen and minerals from bone and connective tissues will be of lower quality than those that contain a larger proportion of muscle meat.

Because inedible food products are not refrigerated or subject to the same handling regulations as are foods destined for human consumption, both the handling and transportation or raw materials can affect the quality of the end product, the meal. If rendering is conducted at the slaughterhouse of origin, the meal is usually produced within a day or two following slaughter. However, when raw materials are transported to a rendering plant in another location, the time spent during transport (and not under refrigerated conditions) can lead to increased microbial contamination and oxidative damage. Differences among rendering plants also exist and are important for the end product. High temperatures or excessively long cooking can damage a meal's protein, making certain essential amino acids less digestible and available.

Finally, as seen with the Blue Buffalo case, pet food companies are at least somewhat dependent upon the integrity and truthfulness of their ingredient suppliers. A division within the animal feed industry designates some meals as pet food grade and others as feed grade, with the former containing a lower percentage of ash (minerals) (5). In addition, some pet food companies select only meals that meet a particular standard while others conduct additional refining methods to their protein meals to increase digestibility and improve protein quality. There are various analytical tests that are used to measure a meal's digestibility and amino acid availability and many pet food companies also routinely measure the digestibility of their foods using feeding trials. However, this information is not easily available to pet owners and pet food companies are under no obligation to accept or reject meals of different quality levels or to share such information with consumers.

Up on my Soapbox

To date, there is no way for pet owners to discern between dry dog foods that use high quality animal protein meals and those that use poor quality meals, other than the cost of the food and the three designators discussed previously. Consumers may opt to contact the company and specifically ask for information about the food's protein digestibility and quality, of course. However, you may be disappointed. While researching my book "*Dog Food Logic*" I contacted the manufacturers of over 30 different pet food brands and requested protein and diet digestibility information for each of the products. I received no reply at all from the majority of companies and useful information from just two of the brands.

Are There Any Other Options? In today's innovative market place, there are a few. Two other animal-source protein ingredients (in addition to fresh meats prepared at home) are those that are either freeze-dried or dehydrated. Freeze-dried ingredients are typically used in raw food diets, but can also be cooked prior to packaging. Dehydration usually uses heat treatment to kill microbial growth and so moderately cooks the meat. These sources are likely to be of higher quality and digestibility because they have not undergone the high heat processing that meals are subjected to. If they are human-grade meats, all the better, as this means the ingredients and end-product were handled and produced using the same regulatory oversight as are required with human foods.

However, with a few exceptions, neither freeze-dried nor dehydrated meat sources are routinely used as the primary protein source in dry, extruded foods. Nor have I found a source of dried protein meals that are produced using human grade (i.e. edible) meat sources and human food processing methods. To do so (and to promote these as such) would add a dimension of choice and distinction regarding the quality of dry dog food that does not exist today. I suggest that since dry dog foods continue to be the most popular type of dog food that is sold in the US, such products would be welcomed by owners who are willing to pay a bit more for a better regulated and higher quality dog food.

While rendered animal meals can be of high quality and can provide an excellent protein source in dry dog foods, if an animal-source meal has been poorly sourced, handled, processed, or regulated, its protein can be damaged, making it a poor source of essential amino acids for dogs and reducing the digestibility and quality of the entire diet. *Unfortunately, there is no way for dog owners to discern from a food's label if the meal that is included is of high, moderate or low quality.* Because meals make up the bulk of protein in dry dog foods, information about their quality (and ability to nourish our dogs) is the most important consideration that we should be concerned with when we look at an ingredient list.

The problem is, consumers have no way of knowing which chicken meals (or any other type of meal) are better than others, despite what companies that are beating the *"No By-Products"* drum would like us to believe.

Cited References:

1. Association of American Feed Control Officials. *2010 Official Publication; Official Feed Definitions*; 2010; pp. 326-322.

2. Aldrich CG, Daristotle L. Pet food and the economic impact. *Proc. California Animal Nutrition Conference*, Fresno, CA. 1998; pp. 1140-1148.

3. Locatelli ML, Howhler D. Poultry byproduct meal: Consider protein quality and variability. *Feed Management* 2003; 54:6-10.

4. Cramer KR, Greenwood MW, Moritz JS. Protein quality of various raw and rendered by-products commonly incorporated into companion animal diets. *Journal of Animal Science* 2007; 85:3285-3293.

5. Dozier WE, Dale NM, Dove CR. Nutrient composition of feed-grade and pet-food-grade poultry by-product meal. *Journal of Applied Poultry Research* 2003; 12:526-530.

5
Want Flies with that Shake?

A potential new protein ingredient for dog foods.
So, how do you feel about bugs?

Well, not actually you, but rather your dog.

Before foodies get up in arms over this topic, consider that numerous human cultures have historically viewed insects as acceptable and even highly desirable food items. And today, our ever-expanding human population plus the increasing need for sustainable sources of food have led to increased consideration of insects as food in almost all human cultures.

So, it's not much of a jump to ask - what might this mean for feeding dogs?

It's all about the Protein: Protein is the most expensive nutrient in the diet of all animals, including humans. It is expensive both in terms of the monetary cost of its production and its ecological impact upon the environment. In the spirit of sustainability (a buzzword that pet food companies and other corporations love to trot out) and with the goal of reduced production costs (i.e. making foods more cheaply), pet nutritionists at Mars-owned Nutro Company recently identified a number of potential alternative protein ingredients for dog and cat foods. Bugs, being plentiful, cheap, and protein-replete were included on the list.

And Protein is All about Amino Acids: Although we talk about a dog's protein requirement and about a food's protein level or quality, the actual requirement that dogs and all animals have is for the essential amino acids (the building blocks of the dietary protein) and the nitrogen that dietary protein supplies. The reason that the parlance of nutrition centers on dietary protein is simply because foods contain protein, not individual amino acids. It is during the process of digestion that a food's protein is broken down in the small intestine into its component amino acids, which are then absorbed into the body. So, at the level of an animal's metabolic needs, it is the amino acids that actually count. This is why one of the first steps that nutritionists take when examining a potential protein-containing ingredient is to examine its amino acid composition.

So, the question in this case is: Can insect protein supply all of the essential amino acids that dogs require? The nutritionists at Nutro collaborated with researchers at the University of California at Davis to find out (1).

The Study: A wide variety of different plant, algae and insect species were identified as potential alternative (and sustainable) protein sources for pet foods. Within the group of insects, the researchers focused on the adult and larval forms of various species of flies, cockroaches, and ants.

All of the bug samples were analyzed for total protein and amino acid content. (I will spare you the details regarding sample acquisition and preparation in case you are reading this during your lunch hour). Amino acid analysis included measurement of the 10 essential amino acids plus taurine, a special type of amino acid that is found primarily in animal tissues. Many readers are probably familiar with taurine as an essential dietary nutrient for cats. Because there is evidence that taurine may be needed during periods of physiological stress in some dogs, it has recently been classified as a "conditional essential amino acid" for dogs as well. Because sources of taurine are limited, it is an important essential nutrient to measure when considering new ingredients for dog and cat foods.

Results: Larval and adult forms of five different insect species were analyzed. Here are their primary findings:

- **High in protein:** Total protein levels in all of the insect species were quite high. When reported on a dry matter basis, concentrations ranged between from 46% in Black Soldier Fly larvae to 96% in cockroaches. (Cockroaches? Who knew?).

- **Bugs can do it:** All but one species of insect (Black Soldier Fly larvae) were found to contain sufficient concentrations of protein, essential amino acids, and taurine to meet or exceed the NRC requirements for growth for dogs and cats. The finding for taurine was rather surprising because it has been previously assumed that rich sources of taurine included only skeletal muscle and organ meats.

- **Ants and flies are best:** Two groups of insects, ants and adult flesh flies, contained the most concentrated sources of taurine. However, these initial results suggest that all three of the groups that were studied - ants, cockroaches, and flies - may be nutritionally acceptable protein sources for dog and cat diets.

Take Away for Dog Folks: Dogs and cats (like humans) require *nutrients* in their diet, not ingredients. Therefore, if a particular protein ingredient can supply most or all of the dog's essential amino acids, is nutritious when fed, and is safe and palatable, then it technically meets the criteria (ick factor aside) to be considered as a potential dietary ingredient. Having passed the first test of adequate protein and amino acid content, where do insects fall on these other criteria?

- **Nutritious when fed:** This refers to how digestible and bioavailable the essential nutrients of the ingredient actually are, when fed to the dog. For example, some insects and plants contain anti-nutritional factors, compounds that interfere with the ability to digest or use certain nutrients. Some of these compounds can be toxic or so potent as to cause illness, making their presence a clear "*no-fly zone*" for pets (pun intended).

- **Safety:** Many species of bugs have ways to protect themselves from becoming someone's meal. They produce toxins that cause illness or consume plants whose by-products are toxic to animals. They may also just taste really, really nasty. Clearly, toxic bugs are out.

- **Acceptability:** Living with four dogs, one of whom is a notorious poop-eater, I would venture that the acceptability issue is as much about the human side of the equation than it is the dog side. Still, dogs must not just accept a bug-flavored food, they must relish it.

Will owners accept it? Might *"Cockroach Recipe for Seniors"* or *"Fly Formula for Active Dogs"* be a hard sell? My (gut) instinct is to say yes, especially in the United States. We all project our own preferences and desires onto our dogs - it is our nature to do so. This is why dog foods that depict entire roasted chickens and sirloin steaks on their front panels sell so well (however misleading such graphics may actually be).

Still, seeing that there is a booming market for dog foods containing alligator meat, brushtail (Australian Possum), and Unagi (freshwater eel), along with treats made from dried bull penises, pig hooves and cow tracheas, one must admit that the bar is already set pretty low. Will insect dog food be next up?

Cited Study: McCuster S, Buff PR, Yu Z, Fascetti AJ. Amino acid content of selected plant, algae and insect species: A search for alternative protein sources for use in pet foods. *Journal of Nutritional Science* 2014;3:e39;1-5.

6
Scoopin' for Science

How important is the digestibility of your dog's food, and how is it measured? Is there perhaps a better way?

I was at the gym recently, swimming laps. After my work-out, I was sitting by the side of the pool and a fellow swimmer and friend stopped to chat about dogs. He has never owned a dog, but his daughter has been pressuring him and he thinks she is finally old enough to take on the responsibility of caring for a dog (good dad!). So, I was anticipating a discussion about breeds, where to look for a dog, training, feeding, etc. But that was not where this was going at all.

Instead, he wanted to talk about poop.

Me: "So, does she have a breed or breed-type that she is considering?"

Him: "No.....not yet. What I really want to ask you about is......the poop thing."

Me: "Um.....what?"

Him: "You know. I see all of the people in our neighborhood taking their dogs for a walk in the morning and they all carry these bags and then, ugh.....they PICK UP THE POOP WITH THEIR HANDS!!!!"

Me: "Well, not exactly; there is a plastic baggie involved. But regardless, what is your point?"

Him: "I just find that so gross and disgusting. I don't think I could do it."

Me: "Wh...What???"

Him: "Ick. Yuck." (Accompanied by a squeamish expression that I have never seen on the face of a grown man).

Me: "Okay, let me get this straight. You are a triathlete. You regularly beat the crap out of your body by swimming, running and cycling ridiculously long distances. You have backpacked and camped all over the country, with no "facilities' and sometimes not bathing for days......and you squirm at picking up dog poop in a plastic baggie?"

Him: "Yeah, that about covers it."

Me (laughing): "You gotta get over that dude. Take a class or something. All dog folks pick up poop. It's no big deal."

Him: "Hmmm....." (not buying it).

It really is no big deal. Many dog owners are not only comfortable with poop scooping, we also regularly examine the quality of our dog's leavings as a general barometer of both their health and the quality of the food that we are feeding.

So, when I learned of a recent study that asked a group of dog owners to do some "poop scoopin' for science" I was only surprised that there have not been more studies of this nature published in the past.

The Issue: If you have read my nutrition book, *Dog Food Logic*, you know that I personally advocate for increased transparency in the pet food industry and for the need to provide dog owners with information that is actually useful to us for selecting foods. Without question, one of the most important measures of a food's quality is its digestibility - the proportion of the food that a dog's gastrointestinal tract is able to actually break down (digest) and absorb into the body for use. Digestibility correlates well with a food's ingredient quality and proper food processing techniques, so this information would be very helpful for dog owners to have. However, the vast majority of companies do not provide it. The only (very rough) estimate of food digestibility that we have is that gleaned by regularly examining the quality and quantity of our dog's feces. A behavior that, in addition to providing very little real information, lends itself to weird looks from neighbors such as my swimming friend. A crappy state of affairs, indeed.

Industry's Position: When challenged, representatives of the pet food industry generally deflect criticism by maintaining that current AAFCO regulations do not require that they report their product's digestibility. (The old *"we don't gotta so we ain't gonna"* defense). Further, not all pet food companies regularly measure digestibility because doing so requires them to conduct feeding trials with dogs which in turn requires access to research kennels and laboratories. Such studies are expensive and may be cost prohibitive for some of the smaller companies that do not maintain their own kennels or in-house analytical laboratories.

Fair enough. However, what about using dogs who live in homes? Why not enlist everyday Citizen Scientists who are dedicated to their dogs, feed commercial dog food, are concerned about quality, and who do not squirm at picking up dog poop? Not only would this lead to increased numbers of dogs enrolled in these trials (thus improving the accuracy of digestibility estimates), it would also allow needed comparisons among breeds, ages, life styles and activity levels of dogs, and could get information about food quality out to the consumers who need it. Another definite advantage of in-home studies is that they lead to reducing the need for kenneled research dogs, a clear animal welfare benefit.

Happily for us, a group of researchers from two universities in The Netherlands were thinking the same thing (1).

The Study: The objective of their study was to develop a simple method of measuring dog food digestibility that could be used with privately owned dogs living in homes. They recruited a group of 40 adult, healthy dogs and asked their owners to feed a test food (and nothing else) for a period of 7 days. Amounts to feed each dog were pre-measured and the volume the dog consumed each day was recorded. In this study, the test diet was a commercial dry (extruded) food formulated for adult dogs. After seven days of feeding, the owners were asked to collect all of their dog's feces for a period of 24-hours. The feces were frozen and submitted to the researchers for analysis.

On the following page is a flow-chart showing how a digestibility trial works. It is conducted in the same manner with kenneled dogs, although feeding and feces collection periods can vary:

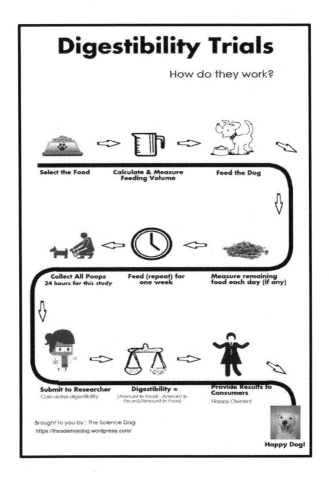

Digestibility Trials

How do they work?

Select the Food — **Calculate & Measure Feeding Volume** — **Feed the Dog**

Collect All Poops 24 hours for this study ← **Feed (repeat) for one week** ← **Measure remaining food each day (if any)**

Submit to Researcher
Calculates digestibility

Digestibility =
(Amount in Food - Amount in feces)/Amount in Food

Provide Results to Consumers
Happy Owners!

Brought to you by : The Science Dog
https://thesciencedog.wordpress.com/

Happy Dog!

Results: The owners recorded the amount of food that their dog consumed each day and collected all of their dog's feces over the final 24-hours of the study. The researchers then analyzed the nutrient content in the food that was consumed and in the feces that were excreted. From these data, they calculated the proportion of the food that each dog digested, called a "digestibility coefficient" and average values for the entire sample of dogs. In this experiment, the food's dry matter digestibility was 77.4 % and its protein digestibility was 77.7 %, values that reflect a food of "low to moderate" quality. The variability among dogs (as reflected by the standard errors), was found to be low. This suggests that the dogs in the trial showed consistency in their ability to digest the food and supports the in-home trial as a valid procedure. In addition, the study reported compliance in 39 out of 40 homes, demonstrating some pretty dedicated poop scooping.

Up on my Soapbox

Up on the Ol' Box: Another recent study evaluated a set of eight commercial dog foods using both nutrient analysis and a set of feeding trials like the one above, but with kenneled dogs (2). They found a very wide range in the overall (dry matter) digestibilities and protein digestibilities among the eight products and noted that these differences would *not* be reflected by information that was provided on the pet food labels. The authors went even further, stating: "...*we have to note that there is no comprehensive list of information available to the consumer to evaluate the quality of commercial diets. A combination of laboratory analyses and estimation of digestibility coefficients is the **only** way to perform an accurate and complete evaluation of the quality of a commercial diet*" And yet, not all pet food companies supply complete nutrient levels for their foods and no pet food companies regularly provides digestibility coefficients to dog owners.

The results of this pilot study tell us that in-home studies with owned dogs can provide needed information about dog food quality and can allow the study of factors that may influence how well dogs utilize different foods, such as age, breed, size, health status and activity levels. Compliance was very good; these owners were willing to do their part, scooping poop for science. Now all that we need is for pet food companies to step up and begin to do their part – to conduct in-home digestibility studies and make the information that they provide available to the dog folks who care.

Cited Studies:

1. Hagen-Plantinga EA, Bosch G, Hendriks WH. Practical approach to determine apparent digestibility of canine diets. *Journal of Nutritional Science* 2014; 3;e31:1-4.

2. Daumas C, Paragon BM, Thorin C, Martin L, Dumon H, Ninet S, Nguyen P. Evaluation of eight commercial dog diets. *Journal of Nutritional Science* 2014;3;e63:1-5.

7
How Reactive is Your Lysine?

Digestibility is one measure of food and protein quality.
Another is measuring a food's reactive lysine content.
Why aren't manufacturers using it?

I imagine that the word "*reactive*" caused most readers to think of this:

However, what we will actually be talking about is this:

$$H_3\overset{+}{N} - \overset{\overset{\displaystyle H}{|}}{\underset{\underset{\displaystyle NH_2}{\underset{|}{(CH_2)_4}}}{\overset{\alpha}{C}}} - C\overset{\displaystyle O}{\underset{\displaystyle O}{}}$$

LYSINE - AN ESSENTIAL AMINO ACID

Yeah, not quite so dramatic, I'll admit. However, the reality is that the amount of reactive lysine present in your dog's food is much more likely to have an impact on his health and wellness

50

than is the somewhat lower risk of meeting Mr. Crabby Pants pictured above.

The reason? Well, it's all about the protein quality of commercial dog foods - the good, the bad, and the reactive.

Reactive Lysine: Lysine is one of the 10 essential amino acids (the building blocks of proteins) that must be provided in a dog's diet. The term *essential* means that dogs cannot produce these amino acids endogenously (in the body) and so they must be supplied by the protein in the food. Of the essential amino acids, lysine is rather unique in that it has a reactive amino group (the H3N+ in the graphic above). This portion of the molecule hangs out into space waving its H+ around, which is ready and able to engage and link up with other molecules. And, just as with reactive dogs, these encounters do not always end well.

When food proteins are subjected to heat treatment and other processing conditions, some of this lysine binds to certain sugars and amino acids. When this occurs, the modified form of lysine is not available, meaning that the dog is unable to use the lysine, even after it has been digested and absorbed into the body. Some of the altered lysine may be modified further to produce compounds called "*advanced Maillard compounds*". Maillard products are actually quite well-known to most people - they cause the browning of the toast that you eat for breakfast, on the onions that you caramelize, and form the grill lines on your hamburger.

Reactive Lysine in Dog Foods: Tasty toast aside, measuring the amount of reactive lysine and Maillard compounds that are present in a dog food provides a reliable indicator of the food's protein quality. This goes above and beyond digestibility (which we discussed previously in "*Scoopin' for Science*"), because the amount of reactive lysine reflects the actual nutritive value of the protein once it has been digested and absorbed into the body.

Processing Damages Protein: The heat treatment that is used to produce commercial dog foods has many benefits - it functions to improve a food's overall digestibility, enhances shelf life, and assures food safety. However, heat and mechanical processing can also result in damage to the food's protein. The good news is that the degree of this damage can be measured using laboratory procedures that analyze reactive (available) lysine (RL) and total lysine (TL). A ratio is then calculated between these two values (RL:TL). A high ratio value reflects more reactive lysine, less protein damage and higher quality protein. Conversely, a low value signifies greater loss of lysine during processing, more damage to the protein, and lower quality. Therefore, a high value is good; a low value is bad.

Cool, Right? Well, yeah. Really cool. Because measuring reactive lysine ratios provides us (dog folks) with an indication of how processing such as canning, extrusion, rendering, and even dehydration or freeze-drying, might damage food protein and reduce the overall quality and nutritional value of a dog food.

Too bad this information is never reported by pet food companies. (To date, they are not required to report any measures of food digestibility or protein quality to their consumers).

Even though pet food manufacturers are not reporting these values, a group of scientists have been.

The Study: Researchers with the Animal Nutrition Group at Wageningen University in The Netherlands have been examining reactive lysine content and Maillard reaction products in a variety of commercial pet foods. In a recent paper, they collected 67 different brands of dog and cat foods, formulated for different life stages (1). Lysine levels were measured for each, and RL:TL ratios were calculated. The researchers also compared available lysine levels in the foods to the minimum lysine requirements reported by the current *NRC Nutrient Requirements for Dog and Cats.*

Results: A wide range of RL:TL ratios were reported, suggesting that protein damage in commercial foods is highly variable and may not be dependent simply on the type of processing that is used:

- **Processing type vs. ingredients:** Overall, as reflected by the RL:TL ratio, canned foods had less protein damage than extruded foods, which had less damage (surprisingly) than pelleted foods. However, the range of values *within* processing type was very high with the three types of foods showing a lot of overlap. This suggested that source and type of ingredients may matter as much as or even more than processing type.

- **Ingredients:** Many of the ingredients that are used to produce pelleted and extruded foods are pre-treated with heat, drying and grinding. For extruded foods, this refers primarily to the production of meat meals (see "*What's the Deal with Meals*" for a complete discussion of protein meals). It is speculated that this processing and how well it is (or is not) controlled is the most important determinant of changes in protein quality.

- **Meeting lysine requirements:** Of the foods that were examined in this study, up to 23 percent of a product's lysine could be damaged and made unavailable to the dog. When these losses were considered while accounting for expected protein/lysine digestibility, some of the foods were expected to be at risk to not meet the minimum lysine requirement for growing dogs.

The authors conclude: "*Ingredients and pet foods should be characterized with respect to their reactive lysine content and digestibility, to avoid limitations in the lysine supply to growing dogs*" I would add to this that these measures should be available in some form to consumers, as a measure of the protein quality of the food that they are considering buying.

Detractors might argue that RL:TL ratio is "*too complex*" for consumers to process and understand. I disagree. A simple classification chart, such as "poor, moderate, and high" quality could be derived from the range of reactive lysine values that are reported. Knowing this information, along with the type and source of ingredients, would allow owners to make meaningful quality distinctions among foods.

Draggin' out the Box

I have argued in *Dog Food* Logic (and in the previous essay) that pet food producers should be required to provide digestibility information about their products, when requested. This is not too much to ask, seeing that manufacturer's claims of "*Complete and Balanced*" promotes the feeding of their products as the sole source of nutrition to our dogs. And now, according to the results of research coming from Wageningen University, there are additional measures of protein quality that can differentiate among poor, adequate and superior foods.

It is time to ask for more of pet food manufacturers. Measuring digestibility and reactive lysine levels of foods provide measures of quality that are directly pertinent to a food's nutritive value and to our dogs' health. If we are asked to buy into the "complete and balanced" claim, then we are entitled to ask for evidence that a food actually meets those claims.

Cited Study: van Rooijen C, Bosch G, van der Poel AFB, Wierenga PA, Alexander L, Hendriks WH. Reactive lysine content in commercially available pet foods. *Journal of Nutritional Science* 2104; 3:e35:1-6.

8
Keep Those Doggies Rollin'...
Rawhide, Rawhide!

Let's talk about dog chews and treats. How digestible are those chews and rawhides that many dogs love so much?

A dog person cannot walk into a pet supply store (or their own grocery store, for that matter) without noticing the explosion in the number of dog chews, dental devices and edible bones that are available for sale today. Some of these are baked biscuits or extruded concoctions containing a mixture of ingredients, while others originate from cow skin (rawhide chews) or are the left-over body parts of a hapless food animal (pig/lamb ears, hooves, tracheas, and bully sticks).

Even as the selection of these items has expanded, nutritional information about them is still glaringly absent. Since all of these products are intended to be chewed slowly so that pieces or the entire produce will be gradually consumed by the dog, we should at least be informed as to whether these items can actually be digested, should we not?

Are They Digestible? Dry matter digestibility refers to the proportion of a food that a dog's gastrointestinal tract is capable of breaking down (digesting) and absorbing into the body. When discussing the digestibility of a dog *food*, we are primarily concerned with its nutrient value and ability to nourish the dog. However, when we are considering the digestibility of rawhide treats, chews and dental products, the concerns are different but equally important. Any portion of a chew that is broken off and swallowed will travel through the length of a dog's gastrointestinal tract, just like any other food. And, if the dog is able to bite off large chunks or swallow an entire chew at once, that piece has the potential to cause digestive upset, impede normal gut motility, or in the worse-case scenario, cause obstruction if it is not dissolved and digested as it moves along.

Recently, a team of researchers at the University of Illinois decided to examine exactly this question by comparing the digestibility of different types of dog chews.

The Studies: Two studies were conducted, both using an *in vitro* (test tube) technique that has been validated as a measure of the digestive conditions that occur in a dog's stomach (gastric digestion) and small intestine (intestinal digestion). The first study compared the *in vitro* dry matter digestibility values of sample products from six broad categories of dog treats (1). All of the products that were tested were produced by Hartz Mountain Corporation and the study was funded by the company. The second study compared just two types of treats, pork skin versus beef rawhide chews (2). The researchers also measured digestibility of the pork skin chew using a feeding trial with dogs. (For an explanation of digestibility trials with dogs, see essay *"Scoopin' for Science"*). The reason for not doing a feeding study with the beef rawhide chew was not explained in the paper.

Results: Together, the two studies reported several interesting differences between the digestibilities of different types of dog chews:

1. **Pig ears:** Chews made from pig's ears, which are composed primarily of cartilage and the structural protein collagen had very low gastric (stomach) digestibilities (14 %). Although these were almost completely digested in the intestinal environment (90 %), the lack of change in gastric acid means that a pig's ear treat, if swallowed, would potentially leave the stomach intact and enter the small intestine will little change in size and consistency.

2. **Rawhide chews:** Similarly, with the exception of one product, rawhide chews made from cow skin were very poorly digested in the stomach. Intestinal digestion was almost complete for one product, but others continued to have low digestibility, even in the intestinal environment. *The researchers noted that feeding rawhide chews to a dog who tended to consume large pieces could increase a dog's risk for intestinal blockage.*

3. **Pork skin vs. rawhide:** When a pork skin chew was compared directly to a beef rawhide chew, the pork skin product's digestibility was significantly greater than that of beef rawhide chew. After six hours, which is approximately the time it takes for a meal to begin to leave a dog's stomach and enter the small intestine, the pork chew was more than 50 percent digested, while the rawhide was only 7.6 percent digested. This low rate of gastric break down continued even when tested up to 24 hours. After simulation of digestion in the small intestine (the major site of digestive processes in dogs), the pork skin rawhide was almost 100 % digested, while the beef rawhide reached only 50 to 70 % digestion under the same conditions. Rawhide was digested up to 85 % only when exposed to the intestinal conditions for 24 hours.

4. **Feeding study:** When dogs were fed one pork skin chew per day along with their normal diet, the overall digestibility of the diet increased. This corroborates the *in vitro* results and supports the conclusion that the pork skin chews were highly digestible.

Take Away for Dog Folks: One of the most interesting results of these studies was the finding of such a large difference between the digestibilities of pork skin versus beef rawhide chews. Because some dogs consume these types of chews rapidly and swallow large chunks, the fact that pork chews but not beef rawhides are highly degraded in the stomach and are highly digestible overall, is of significance to dog owners. These data suggest that if an owner is going to feed some type of rawhide chew (and mind you, I am not advocating for feeding these types of treats), but if one was choosing and had a dog who might consume the treat rapidly, feeding a pork skin chew appears to be a safer bet than a beef rawhide chew.

Second, it is important to note that all types of rawhide-type chews are composed of collagen, a structural protein that makes up most of the connective tissues in the body. This is true for ears, pig skin, rawhide, and yes, even bully sticks. As these data show, collagen can be highly digestible (or not). The difference most likely depends on the source of the product and the type of processing that is used, both of which vary a great deal among chews.

Feeding a dog a chew that is composed of collagen, even when it is highly digestible, does *not* a nutritious treat make. Although collagen is a very important and essential protein in the body, it is not a highly nutritious food protein because it is composed almost completely of non-essential amino acids and is deficient in four of the essential amino acids.

What this means from a practical perspective is that even though certain types of rawhide chews are found to be highly digestible and safe (from a digestibility perspective), this does not mean that they are providing high quality nutrition to the dog. In fact, they do not. While this research is important for pushing the peanut forward regarding the safety of these products in terms of digestibility, effects on gut motility, and risk of blockage, we still need more information (and selection) of chews for dogs that are both digestible *and* nutritious.

CITED STUDIES:

1. de Godoy MRC, Vermillion R, Bauer LL, Yamka R, Frantz N, Jia T, Fahey GC Jr, Swanson KS. In vitro disappearance characteristics of selected categories of commercially available dog treats. *Journal of Nutritional Science* 2014; 3:e47;1-4.

2. Hooda S, Ferreira LG, Latour MA, Bauer LL, Fahey GC Jr, Swanson KS. In vitro digestibility of expanded pork skin and rawhide chews, and digestion and metabolic characteristics of expanded pork skin chews in healthy adult dogs. *Journal of Animal Science* 2012; 90:4355-4361.

9
Got Gullet?

Are gullets and tracheae treats safe for dogs to consume? Evidence shows that they may not be - if the thyroid gland came along for the ride.

Innovative dog chews and treats are all the rage these days. Despite the claims of their sellers, most of these products are new twists on an old theme - taking the parts of food animals that we typically discard as inedible waste and turning them into expensive and often highly sought after dog treats. A few examples are bully sticks, pig ears, pig/cow hooves, cod skins, and the topic of this essay, beef gullets (esophagus) and tracheae. In addition to coming in a dried form as a chew, the entire neck regions of beef, lamb, chicken, turkey and other food animals are also included in some commercial and homemade raw diets.

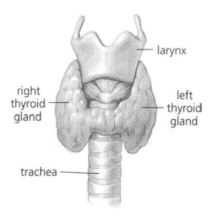

Quick Anatomy Lesson: The thyroid gland is a small organ that wraps around the upper portion of an animal's trachea (wind pipe). When a cow is dissected for the production of human-grade meat, the trachea and esophagus are removed together as by-products. Although a law passed in 1986 prohibits their inclusion in human foods, these animal parts *can* be used in pet foods, which is exactly where they end up (along with other animal by-products that are deemed not for human consumption).

Thyroid Tissue in Your Dog's Food: Thyroid tissue contains the hormone thyroxine, which will not be destroyed by the dog's gastric acid or digestive enzymes. It is absorbed into the body and remains active. If a dog consumes enough thyroxine, an elevation in circulating thyroid hormone occurs and the dog develops hyperthyroidism (or more technically correct, thyroid-toxicosis). Some dogs develop elevated serum thyroxine but do not show clinical signs. Others develop signs that include weight loss, hyperactivity, excessive panting, and polydipsia/polyuria (increased drinking/urinating).

So, is this a problem that owners should be concerned with? **Possibly; especially if you are feeding a raw diet. Here is the evidence**:

- **Twelve dogs fed raw diets:** In 2012, German veterinarians at Justus Liebig University reported elevated plasma thyroxine levels in dogs who were being fed either a raw diet or large amounts of fresh or dried beef gullet (1). Clinical signs of hyperthyroidism were reported in half of the dogs (6/12). Following diagnosis, seven owners immediately switched to a commercial dry food and stopped feeding gullet. Veterinary rechecks 2 weeks and 2 months later revealed that plasma thyroxine concentrations had returned to normal and clinical signs had resolved in all of the dogs. One owner did not change her dog's diet. Repeated thyroid hormone tests showed elevated levels one and four months following diagnosis and the dog was experiencing chronic weight loss. At that point, the owner switched the dog to another food, clinical signs resolved and plasma thyroxine levels returned to normal.

- **Two additional cases:** Two more cases were reported in 2014. In the first, an 11-month-old male Rottweiler was examined for signs of weight loss, excessive panting and increased blood thyroxine levels (2). A complete diet history revealed that the dog was being fed a commercial raw diet. After switching the dog to a commercial dry food, signs resolved and blood thyroxine levels returned to normal. In a second case study, a two-year-old female Miniature Pinscher was examined for a failure to come into estrus (3). The dog was fed a homemade raw diet that included beef cuts from the head and neck region purchased from a local butcher shop. The dog had highly elevated serum thyroxine levels. Changing the dog's diet led to normalization of serum thyroxine and normal estrus cycles.

- **Raw foods and chews:** Most recently, a study published in the Journal of the American Veterinary Medical Association reported findings of thyroid toxicosis in 14 dogs fed either a commercial raw diet or a variety of different chews or treats (4). All of the treats were some type of sliced or rolled jerky chew. Clinical signs resolved and thyroid hormone levels were normalized within four weeks of discontinuing the suspect products. The authors were able to obtain seven samples of the brands of food or treats that owners were feeding. When tested, all had elevated thyroxine levels when compared with control foods. The authors end with this statement: *"The presence of high T4 concentrations in a variety of pet foods or treats sold under different labels suggests that the problem of thyroid tissue contamination of such items may be widespread and not confined to only a few products or manufacturers."* (The authors also sent samples and identifying information about the products to the FDA for further investigation).

Take Away for Dog Folks: First, let me state up front that these research results are by no means presented here as a personal vendetta against feeding raw. If you have read *Dog Food Logic* you will know that my position regarding raw feeding is that there are many approaches to feeding dogs healthfully, and a well-balanced, properly selected (and *sourced*) raw diet can be one of those approaches.

However, the evidence that I review here strongly suggests that the recent increase in diet-induced hyperthyroidism is likely a result of the increased popularity of both raw diets and of feeding unusual types of chews such as gullets and tracheae to dogs. At the very least, this set of case studies provides sufficient evidence that diet-induced hyperthyroidism is a health risk that warrants further study and investigation of the identified companies and brands.

Up on My Soapbox

Draggin' Out the Ol' Box: Fear not. I do have a personal opinion on this matter (though I would be hesitant to go so far [yet] as to call it a vendetta). This has to do with data reported in the 2015 study, which were collected in the United States. In that study, all 14 of the dogs were being fed *commercially prepared foods* at the time of diagnosis. These were foods that the owners purchased from a company, trusting that the products would not only provide good nutrition to their dogs, but that they were **safe**. This should not be such a high bar to clear, yet it repeatedly seems to be so for some members of the pet food industry.

Here's the Thing: The knowledge that the presence of animal thyroid tissue in foods can cause hyperthyroidism is not new information. Outbreaks of diet-induced hyperthyroidism in people are well-documented and are the reason that "gullet trimming" as a source of ground beef was outlawed in the 1980's. Yet, these tissues are still allowed in the foods that we feed to our companion animals. Why is this?

I maintain that pet owners should be able to easily discover exactly what is in the pet foods they feed to their dogs, including the source and quality of the product's protein ingredients. Yet this information is rarely provided and requests for it are often ignored, denied or responded to with evasive platitudes and assurances. Here's a suggestion - Ask your pet food manufacturer if the food that you feed contains animal necks and if they guarantee that it does not contain thyroid tissue. If they cannot provide such a guarantee, switch to another food.

In a perfect world (and when I am Queen), we will ban the inclusion of unsafe body parts in the foods that we feed to our canine family members. I know it is an outrageous suggestion, but a person can dream, cant' she?

Got gullet? Let's hope not.

Cited References:

1. Kohler B, Stengel C, Neiger R. Dietary hyperthyroidism in dogs. *Journal of Small Animal Practice* 2012; 523:182-184.

2. Cornelissen S, De Roover K, Paepe D, Hesta M, Van der Meulen E, Daminet S. Dietary hyperthyroidism in a Rottweiler. *Vlaams Diergeneeskundig Tijdschrift* 2014; 83:306-311.

3. Sontas BH, Schwendenwein I, Schafer-Somi S. Primary anestrus due to dietary hyperthyroidism in a Miniature Pinscher bitch. *Canadian Veterinary Journal* 2014; 55:781-785.

4. Broome MR, Peterson ME, Kemppainen RJ, Parker VJ, Richter KP. Exogenous thyrotoxicosis in dogs attributable to consumption of all-meat commercial dog food or treats contain-

ing excessive thyroid hormone: 14 cases (2008-2013). *Journal of the American Animal Hospital Association* 2015; 246:105-111.

10
"Does This Collar Make Me Look Fat?"

Said no dog. Ever.

As dog owners, it is our responsibility to keep our dogs at a healthy body weight and in good condition. We all know this, right?

Perhaps not. A few statistics:

- Obesity continues to be the *number one* nutritional problem in pet dogs in the United States.

- According to the Association of Pet Obesity Prevention (APOP), veterinarians classified *53 percent* of their canine patients as either overweight or obese.

- In the same survey, only *22 percent of the owners* identified their dog as being overweight.

- APOP founder Dr. Ernie Ward refers to this cognitive disconnect as the *"fat pet gap"*. He suggests that American dog owners' perceptions of what is normal in their dogs has been gradually distorted, leading to the perception that an overweight body type is normal.

Why the Disconnect? A common theory used to explain the mismatch between what owners *perceive* and what their dog actually *looks* like is that owners simply have not been taught how to recognize a fat dog and that they lack the knowledge to differentiate between a dog who is at ideal weight versus one who is slightly (or more) overweight. In an attempt to counteract this problem, pet food companies created Body Condition Scores. These are standardized five to 9-point visual scales designed to help owners and veterinarians correctly assess a dog's body condition.

Problem Solved? These scales have been around for more than 15 years. Yet, our dogs are still fat, and appear to be getting fatter. Perhaps the scales are not being used? Are they difficult to understand? Recently a group of researchers asked the question: "*If we give dog owners a BCS tool, show them how to use it, and then ask them to evaluate their own dog using the tool, will their assessments improve?*" Their hypothesis was optimistic. They believed this would do the trick.

The Study: This was a pre-test/post-test study design and included a group of 110 owners and their dogs (1). In the pre-test portion of the study, owners were asked to assess their dog's body condition. No guidance was provided and the owner was required to select the word that best described their dog from a set of five terms. These were: very thin, thin, ideal weight, overweight, or markedly obese. Following this assessment, the owner was provided with a five-point BCS chart that used the same five descriptors along with visual silhouettes and complete descriptions. They were given instructions of how to use the chart and were then asked to assess their dog a second time. The investigating veterinarian also assessed the dog using the BCS chart and via a physical examination.

Results: Several interesting (and surprising) results were reported:

1. Prior to using the BCS chart, 2/3 of the owners (66 %) incorrectly assessed their dog's body condition. The majority of those who were incorrect *underestimated* body condition, believing their overweight dog to be at or near his or her ideal weight. These results are consistent with those reported by other researchers and with the APOP survey.

2. Following training with the BCS tool, these misperceptions persisted, showing virtually no change; 65 % of the owners were incorrect and only 15 % changed their original score (some up/some down, and some from correct to incorrect!). *The majority of owners continued to see their plump dog as being at his or her optimal weight.*

3. Here is where things get really weird.

   - When queried, the majority of owners (77 %) stated that they believed that using the BCS chart had significantly improved their ability to estimate their dog's body condition (huh?). This statement was made despite the fact that only 17 owners changed their scores after they learned to use the chart.

   - And, those who believed the chart had helped them fared no better in post-test success than those who believed that the chart did not help them.

Take Away for Dog Folks: This study confirms what several other researchers have reported and what the APOP statistics tell us; dog owners tend to underestimate their dog's weight and body condition, and tend to perceive a dog who is overweight as ideal. It also goes an important step further. Even when owners are shown how to identify an overweight dog, they are literally blind to seeing the evidence in their own dog. We *still* get it wrong. Why is this happening? There are a few possible reasons:

- **Fido is not fat; he just has big bones:** Resistance to seeing one's own dog as overweight may be a form of denial, similar to the well-documented misperception that many parents have regarding their child's weight. Because being overweight is viewed negatively by others, is associated with well-known health risks, and may be perceived as reflecting badly upon a dog owner's ability to care properly for their dog, denial may be quite an attractive alternative to the truth.

- **Confirmation bias:** In this pre-test/post-test situation, people may have resisted changing their scores following training simply because, well, people hate to admit that they were wrong. If an owner had preconceived beliefs about his dog's weight and initially assigned a moderate score, he might subsequently (and unconsciously) use the BCS chart to confirm that belief, however misguided it was.

- **Food is love:** There are data from other studies showing that a substantial number of owners admit that they are unwilling to deny food to their dog even when they know the dog is overweight because they see feeding as an important outlet for love and nurturing (2). Similarly, owners tend to resist changing their feeding habits with their dogs even when aware of the adverse health effects of being overweight (3).

Up on my Soapbox

Soap Box Time: The results of this study are not encouraging and suggest that we have a long way to go regarding our ability to prevent and reduce overweight conditions in dogs. If you are a trainer, doggy day care owner, groomer, veterinarian, veterinary technician, or other pet professional who works daily with dog owners and their dogs, perhaps it is time for a little "tough love". Post a BCS chart in your facility, have a weight scale handy, and don't be afraid to use it. Call the fat dogs fat.......nicely of course and with great respect for their owners (the dogs won't care; they will be proud). Help owners to face reality. Provide guidelines to help dogs to trim down, encourage exercise for both the dog's body and mind, and help people to understand that keeping a dog trim is one of the best ways that we can support their health and demonstrate our love.

Cited Studies:

1. Eastland-Jones RC, German AJ, Holden SL, Biourge V, Pickavance LC. Owner misperception of canine body condition persists despite use of a body condition score chart. *Journal of Nutritional Science* 2014; 3:e45;1-5.

2. Kienzle E, Bergler R, Mandernach A. A comparison of the feeding behavior and the human-animal relationship in owners of normal and obese dogs. *Journal of Nutrition* 1998; 128:2779S-2782S.

3. Bland IM, Guthrie-Jones A, Taylor RD. Dog obesity: Owner attitudes and behavior. *Preventive Veterinary Medicine* 2009; 92:333-340.

11
Weigh In On This

Are veterinarians routinely weighing their patients (and communicating the results to their clients)?

We learned in the previous essay that more than half of the adult dogs in the United States are overweight. The statistics are not encouraging and suggest that this problem continues to worsen. Previously, we learned that owners of overweight dogs have a tendency to incorrectly assess their dog's body condition, almost always underestimating weight and seeing a dog who is overweight as being ideal.

One suggestion to reduce this epidemic of perceptual disconnect is to post canine body condition score (BCS) charts in veterinary clinics. The reasoning is that veterinarians will use these charts to educate their clients and help owners to get a better handle on Rover's weight problems. Of course, such charts are only helpful if the veterinarian chooses to use them and then actually discusses Rover's weight with their client. Therefore, as a follow-up question to this research, one might ask, "*Do veterinarians regularly access the body condition of dogs during routine visits?*" Lucky for us, a group of researchers asked exactly that.

The Study: Private veterinary practices in England, Wales, Scotland and Northern Ireland were recruited to participate. Data from over 49,000 patient visit records were collected and were examined for the inclusion of a weight diagnosis (overweight or obese). When a diagnosis was found in the record, the dog was matched with a control dog using the criteria of age, sex, neuter status, breed and of course, weight. However, the control dog did *not* have a recorded diagnosis of being overweight. This research design is called a "case controlled study" and it allowed the researchers to examine various factors that influence whether or not a veterinarian will focus on a dog's weight status during a routine veterinary visit.

Results: Of the 49,488 dogs whose records were examined, a notation for being overweight was found in only 671 cases (**1.4%** of the dogs). Body condition score was recorded in less than 25 percent of patients. When comparisons were made between the dogs whose record showed a diagnosis of being overweight with their matched controls for which no diagnosis was made, only one health-related factor was found to influence whether or not a veterinarian discussed (and recorded) a dog's overweight status. This was the diagnosis of osteoarthritis or lameness as a presenting problem. The researchers speculated that veterinarians would naturally include a thorough weight assessment in dogs with signs of arthritis, given the well documented association between overweight conditions and mobility problems in dogs. No other individual health problem or lifestyle factor was associated with a discussion of weight status during veterinary consultations.

Take Away for Dog Folks: Since data from multiple sources tell us that upwards of 50 percent of pet dogs are overweight or obese, it appears that, much like dog owners, veterinarians are markedly *under-diagnosing* obesity in their canine patients. It also appears that including BCS charts in examining rooms is not the answer, since veterinarians recorded a body condition score for less than 25 % of their patients. It is important to note that an important limitation of this study was that it was able to examine only written patient records and had no way to review the actual conversations that had occurred between veterinarians and their clients. It is certainly possible that in at least some cases, Fluffy's weight problem was discussed during the visit, but not recorded in her file. However, even if the methodology missed a lot of diagnoses, 1.4 % is still a heck of a long way from 50 %. It is reasonable to assume that a substantial number of the 49,000 dogs in this sample group were overweight but had not been diagnosed as such during their routine veterinary visits.

If veterinarians are not stepping up (as much as they should) and calling Rover rotund, who can? Well the good news is that in this day and age there are many other pet professionals who work with dogs on a daily basis, interact regularly and positively with a multitude of dog owners, and who are completely capable of assessing body condition and weight status in dogs. So, trainers, doggy day care owners, independent pet supply store owners, shelter/rescue professionals, dog walkers, and pet sitters - consider this your call to arms! Help out your clients by educating them regarding good feeding and exercise habits for their dogs, carry a BCS chart with you or post one in your business (better yet, have a scale handy), and gently but firmly encourage your owners to prevent overweight conditions in their dogs to keep them healthy and happy throughout life.

Cited Study: Rolph NC, Noble PJM, German AJ. How often do primary care veterinarians record the overweight status of dogs? *Journal of Nutritional Science*, 2014; 3:e58;1-5.

12
Air – It's What's for Dinner

Every once in a while, I read a paper that makes me scratch my head.

Last week was just such a moment. The paper really needs no introduction. The title says it all: "*Increasing volume of food by incorporating air reduces energy intake*" *[in dogs].*

Let's Talk about Obesity (again): In the first essay of this section, "*Do you think I look fat in this collar?*" I included several statistics regarding the occurrence of obesity in American dogs. It is by far the most commonly diagnosed nutritional disorder in dogs. A substantial number of owners do not recognize overweight conditions in their dogs and even when they do, they are unwilling or unable to comply with weight loss recommendations.

In their search to identify new approaches to weight control (preferably approaches that can be marketed into a new brand of dog food), some pet food companies have looked at the effects of *diluting* food calories. An example that many dog owners are familiar with is increasing dietary fiber. This reduces the number of calories provided in a cup of food. Consuming foods that are high in non-fermentable fibers may also enhance feelings of satiety (fullness) in dogs, although the evidence for this effect is not conclusive. A disadvantage of the high fiber approach is that feeding high levels of dietary fiber causes increased defecation frequency and stool quantity, often producing voluminous poops that are loose and smelly, effects that most owners are generally not looking for in a dog food.

Recently, in their quest to find a canine version of the weight loss Holy Grail, researchers latched on to a nutrient that most of us

74

would probably not even consider when thinking about keeping Muffin trim. (We would not consider it because it is actually not a nutrient).

The Study: A group of researchers at the Royal Canin Research Center, at the National College of Veterinary Medicine in France and at the University of Liverpool in the UK collaborated to study the effects of feeding a dry dog food formulated to contain an increased proportion of air (1). They wanted to determine if there was a satiety-producing effect of adding air to extruded kibbles, thereby increasing the volume that is fed whilst delivering the same (or fewer) number of calories. This is essentially a cheaper version of the "let's add fiber to dog food to dilute its calories" approach.

To understand this concept, consider the density (weight/volume) of a cup of corn meal compared with the density of a cup of air-popped popcorn. Same food; more air in the latter than the former. As a result, the cup of popped corn will contain fewer calories and nutrients than the cup of ground corn meal. When we are talking about extruded (dry) dog food, this idea is quite easy to put into practice because varying extrusion conditions during processing can lead to different degrees of expansion in the end product. Highly expanded kibbles contain more air pockets, will feel lighter (because they are), and will provide fewer calories per cup than a food that has the same nutrient formulation but is less expanded.

The Air-Enhanced Food: The researchers created a test diet that was extruded to include a higher proportion of air than that which is typical. Simply expanding the kibbles to a greater degree and increasing its trapped air pockets resulted in a caloric density that was about half that of the control food. The control diet was a food that contained the same ingredients and nutrient profiles, but less air. The researchers conducted three feeding trials:

- **Experiment 1** measured the length of time that it took dogs to consume a meal that contained increasing proportions of the test diet while still providing the same number of calories. Therefore, because the test food contained less than half of the calories per cup than the control food, the volume of food that was fed more than doubled when the test diet was fed exclusively. **Results:** Not surprisingly, it took dogs longer to eat the larger meals of air-enhanced food than it took them to eat the smaller volume of food that they were given of the control diet. (In other words, it took the dogs longer to eat, um......*more* food). Although this sounds obvious, there is some evidence (in human subjects) that slowing down the rate of eating while consuming the same number of calories enhances satiety by increasing the release and effects of satiety-inducing and appetite-suppressing hormones.

- **Experiment 2** fed the test food and the control food to a group of 10 adult Beagles and used a standard procedure used to measure satiety. This methodology involves offering dogs more food than they are expected to eat in sequential meals spaced one hour apart (kinda like "first breakfast and second breakfast" for Hobbit fans). **Results:** Adding air to food slightly enhanced feelings of satiety in dogs. This means that the dogs consumed a bit less food each day (and fewer calories) of the air-enhanced food when allowed to eat all that they desired than they did when they were fed the control food. This effect is similar to the expectation that consuming a high fiber food will lead to making one feel a bit more full and subsequently to consuming less food overall.

- **Experiment 3** used the same protocol as Experiment 2 and compared the satiety-inducing effects of the test diet with a commercially available adult maintenance dog food. The commercial food provided *more than 3 times the calories per* *cup as the test, air-enhanced food.* **Results:** The results were similar to those of Experiment 2. Adding air (lots of it, by comparison) to a food moderately enhanced feelings of satiety in the dogs. I envision a group of over-stuffed Beagles, burping politely (and repeatedly....it is air after all), and saying *"Really. No. I couldn't eat another bite"*.

The researchers concluded: *"....results from the present study indicate that incorporating air into food provides a strategy to reduce energy [caloric] intake in dogs and, consequently could be a useful strategy for weight management in pets."* They also note that this study did *not* show whether or not dogs would reduce their intake of air-enhanced food to levels that would lead to weight loss nor did it measure effects for more than a few days. They assure us that such research is yet to come.

Up on my Soapbox

Draggin' Out the Ol' Box: Even if it can be shown that increasing the amount of air in a dog's food enhances satiety, do we really need such a food? If one's goals are to reduce a dog's caloric intake and slow rate of eating, there are already effective approaches that owners can take. We can select a high quality food (or home prepared diet) that is well-matched to our dog's lifestyle and activity level. If a dog gains too much weight, we can reduce the amount that is fed or switch to a food that is still of high quality but is lower in fat (i.e. less energy dense without diluting calories). Increasing exercise through daily walks, engaging in a new dog training activity or sport, or teaching retrieve or "find it" games will all burn more calories and help increase a dog's fitness level.

What about Satiety? Is it true that feeding a larger volume of food or slowing the rate of eating will help our dogs to feel more satisfied? Perhaps. There is certainly some evidence to support this theory. However, while the hormonal changes associated with a slower rate of eating may enhance feelings of satiety, do we really need to inject air into our dog's food to accomplish this? Many owners spread out their dog's daily meal time by using a food delivery toy that their dog enjoys or feed using a "slow" bowl that is constructed to make the dog work a bit harder for his food. Providing multiple small meals a day or floating dry food in warm water prior to feeding can also be helpful to slow rate of eating.

Surely, we should not be expected to view injecting air into food as the new miracle weight loss approach for dogs. Are we really destined to see a new brand of dog food on the shelves selling under the marketing slogan of *"Let Them Eat Air"?*

Cited Study: Serisier S, Pizzagalli A, Leclerc L, Feugier A, Nguyen P, Biourge V, German AJ. Increasing volume of food by incorporating air reduces energy intake. *Journal of Nutritional Science* 2104; 3;e59:1-5.

13
The Nature of Natural

Does a claim of "natural" mean anything for your dog or is it just one more marketing gimmick?

Over the last few years, the sale of dog foods that carry a claim of natural, either embedded into their brand name or proclaimed on their front label, has exploded. According to the marketing research firm Packaged Facts, who studies these things, *natural* foods are currently the fastest growing segment of the U.S. pet food market. The sale of foods that are marketed in this way doubled between 2008 and 2012 and accounted for almost 80 percent of all new products introduced between January and August of 2014. Natural pet food sales dollars during the same period exceeded 3 billion dollars, making up two-thirds of total pet food sales.

So, what is all of the fuss about?

What Natural is: The Association of American Feed Control Officials (AAFCO), the organization that sets pet food ingredient and labeling definitions, states that a pet food manufacturer can include the word *natural* in a product's brand name or as a label claim if the food has been preserved using only non-synthetic (i.e. naturally-derived) preservatives. This means that the food cannot include artificially produced compounds such as butylated hydroxyanisole (BHA), butylated hydroxytoluene (BHT), tert-butyl hydroquinone (TBHQ), or ethoxyquin. Instead, naturally-derived preservatives such as tocopherols (vitamin E), ascorbic acid (vitamin C), citric acid, and rosemary extract are used. In today's pet food market, this is not a high bar to clear. Starting in the 1980's, consumer pressure to eliminate the use of ethoxyquin in pet foods was followed by a general trend away from artificial preservatives. Today almost all pet food manufacturers produce at least one product line of foods that are preserved without synthetic compounds and legally carry the "*All Natural*" claim.

In Practice: AAFCO's definition of "natural" is so broad that it includes nearly every single type of pet food ingredient that is currently included in commercial pet foods, with the exception of chemically synthesized vitamins and minerals. And even with these, there is a loop-hole. A manufacturer that includes these items can still use the natural moniker provided the statement "*with added vitamins and minerals*" is tacked onto the natural label claim.

What Natural is Not: A pet food label claim of natural does not signify anything about a food's quality, the source or type of ingredients that it includes, the company's manufacturing practices, or the brand's safety record. Neither does the appearance of the word *natural* signify that a food is organic, that it contains no GMO ingredients, is made from human-grade or high quality ingredients, or does not contain by-products. The bottom line is that other than assuring the owner that the food does not contain synthetic preservatives, a label claim of "*natural*" is meaningless and provides no information that helps to differentiate among foods in terms of their ingredients, quality, digestibility, manufacturing practices or food safety.

Natural vs. Organic: There is however an important distinction between the terms natural and organic. According to the USDA's National Organic Standards Board, a food can be labeled organic if the plant ingredients that are included were grown without pesticides, artificial or sewage sludge fertilizers, or irradiation and exclude genetically modified organisms (GMOs). Animal-source ingredients must come from animals that were raised exclusively on organic feed, were not treated with hormones or antibiotics, and were housed/fed according to an agreed upon welfare standard. However, these requirements were developed for human foods and the National Organic Program (NOP) lacks the legal authority to regulate organic label claims on pet food.

Pet food companies can voluntarily choose to meet the NOP standards, apply for NOP certification, and if accepted can use the USDA Organic seal. However, because certification is optional, a pet food company's use of certified organic ingredients does not mean that the product itself is certified organic via USDA standards. AFFCO has not yet developed a regulation for organic pet foods and recommends that pet food companies attempt to follow the USDA organic food regulations in their labeling practices. However, companies are not required to do so.

If a company chooses to follow the guidelines of the National Organic Program (NOP), you should be able to tell by reading their claim and the ingredients list. If the label states "*100 Percent Organic*", every single ingredient must be organic. Foods labeled simply "*Organic*" must include at least 95 percent organically produced ingredients. Below this level is the label claim "*Made with Organic Ingredients*", for which at least 70 percent of the product's ingredients are organic.

Why Natural? Oddly enough, despite the fact that the term organic is more narrowly defined and better regulated than the term natural, it is the natural foods segment and not organic pet foods that are taking off in sales. A recent marketing research study examined these differences (1).

The Study: Marketing researchers at New Mexico State University surveyed a group of 661 U.S. dog owners regarding their pet food choices. The researchers used a research methodology called "discrete choice analysis" in which they presented participants with a panel of dog foods that varied in key attributes such as price, ingredient type, label claims, and package size and asked them to identify the food that they would choose for their dog. The objectives of the study were to test the effects of label claims such as "*Veterinarian Recommended*", "*Natural*" and

"Organic", as well as package size, life stage formulation, and price upon dog owner preferences. Because a primary goal was to study perceptions of natural pet foods, the participants were provided with the AAFCO's definition of the term natural and the USDA's definition of the term organic prior to starting the survey.

Results: Of the five primary dog food attributes that were studied, the price of the food was found to be the most important determinant of choice. U.S. dog owners were consistently interested in finding the least expensive food. Following product cost, owners focused most intently upon whether or not the food's ingredients were promoted as being natural or organic. When these two ingredient types were compared, dog owners were willing to pay the highest (premium) price for a dog food containing a claim of natural ingredients, more so even than for a food stating that it contained organic ingredients. Other attributes such as being recommended by a veterinarian, life stage formulation, and package size were less important. Following price point, the most important driver for choosing a dog food was seeing the word *"Natural"* somewhere on the label or in the brand name.

Take Away for Dog Folks: Perhaps the most important fact that dog owners should be aware of is that virtually anything goes when it comes to the *"It's Natural"* claim on pet food labels. (This is also true of human foods, by the way). The only significant requirement is that a dog food labeled as "All Natural" has is that it cannot contain artificial preservatives. That's All.

However, even knowing the ridiculously broad definition of the term natural, people continued to attribute great value to the term and showed that they were willing to pay a premium price to see it on their dog's food label. In fact, this study found that owners were willing to pay more for natural ingredients than for organic ingredients despite learning just minutes earlier about the clear differences between the two terms and the stricter guidelines for and regulation of organic foods. Have no doubt about it; this distinction is a win-win for pet food manufacturers because the cost difference between making an "*All Natural*" pet food claim (that means nothing) and an "*Organic*" claim that (though optional) is associated with set guidelines for ingredient production and sourcing, is substantial. Expect to see even more of the word natural on pet food shelves in the future.

And train yourself to ignore that word.

Pet food claims for providing superior nutrition, for promoting health, or for being safer do not follow from a claim of natural-ness without evidence of such benefit. And, this is especially true when the word means nothing at all in the first place.

Cited Study: Simonsen JE, Fasenko GM, Lillywhite JM. The value-added dog food market: Do dog owners prefer natural or organic dog foods? *Journal of Agricultural Science* 2014; 6:86-97.

14
Pet Food Marketing – Science Weighs in

Should you believe the health claims that are made on pet food labels? Should you use these claims to select a food for your dog?

Marketing researchers know a lot about advertising strategies that successfully increase sales. This is no less true for pet foods than it is for any other consumer goods. Some of the more obvious approaches to attracting dog owners to a particular brand are advertisements that appeal to our emotional attachment to dogs, capitalize on our desire for expert approval, or that exploit our fascination with the lives of celebrities.

One of my personal favorites of the "I love celebrities" category is an ingenious brand of Nestle'-Purina's in which the celebrity to whom the product refers, supposedly a famous chef, does not, um, actually *exist*.......

The Ad: *It's not just dog food. It's Chef Michael's. Crafted with great care, attention to detail and inspiration from our executive chef"*

Purina's Disclaimer: In the spirit of full disclosure (and to avoid litigation), the company provides the following response to inquiries about the whereabouts of the personage who is Chef Michael: *"Chef Michael is not a real person, but a reflection of the many people inspired to make mealtime special for their dogs"*. I dunno. I think I would still like to get the guy's autograph.

So, pick your poison - there is a dog food advertising campaign out there designed to appeal to just about every dog owner demographic. And, even though each and every one of us will insist that these schemes do not work on us (and that we select a dog food based solely upon its nutrient content, ingredient quality and suitability for our dog, thank you very much), these campaigns do indeed work very well.

Marketing's Holy Grail: One category of advertising claims that has been shown to work particularly well, increasing human and pet food sales more than any other, are **health claims**. Because of the cumulative effects of a series of three laws that were passed in the 1990's, the regulatory oversight of health claims on foods has been drastically curtailed over the last 35 years. Over time, the loss of regulatory oversight over health claims in human foods has led to human food labels that make a wide and ever expanding range of claims.

Dog Foods Quickly Followed Suit. Pet foods are no different. As it stands today, pet food companies may include general health claims on their labels with no legal obligation to substantiate those claims. *In other words, they neither have to prove the claim nor provide any evidence supporting the claim to any regulatory agency.* Marketers must simply word their brand name or advertisement carefully enough to prevent the FDA from considering it a drug claim (which are monitored and regulated).

The difference between a general health claim (allowed and no proof needed) and a drug claim (not allowed; regulated by FDA) for pet foods turns on just a few words and phrases, as shown in the table below, adapted from my nutrition book, *Dog Food Logic.*

ALLOWED	PROHIBITED (DRUG CLAIM)
• Supports healthy skin and a shiny coat • Promotes a glossy coat	• Reduces skin flaking and itchiness • Prevents skin problems and allergies
• Helps maintain healthy joints and mobility • Glucosamine & chondroitin promote joint and cartilage health	• Reduces signs of arthritis and pain • Prevents progression of joint disease • Reduces joint inflammation
• Supports a healthy immune system • Contains antioxidants for immune system health	• Improves your dog's immune response • Prevents infection by supporting the immune system
• Promotes oral health; keeps teeth clean • Controls tartar build-up on teeth	• Prevents dental problems such as gingivitis and periodontal disease • Treats gum disease
• Supports a healthy gastrointestinal tract • Promotes efficient digestion	• Prevents digestive and intestinal problems • Improves digestion in sensitive dogs

Table Adapted from *Dog Food Logic*, by Linda P. Case, Dogwise, 2014.

Might these health claims be confusing to pet owners? A recent study asked exactly that question.

The Study: A group of researchers at Tufts University's Cummings School of Veterinary Medicine examined the nutrient profiles and ingredients list of 24 brands of dog food that all were marketed for skin and coat health (1). The objective of their study was to identify consistencies (or inconsistencies) among different commercial products making claims of promoting skin and coat health in dogs.

Results: They examined 15 dry (extruded) foods and 9 canned foods, representing 11 different brand names. Here are their results:

- *It's all in the name:* All 24 products included the terms skin and coat plus a descriptor of skin/coat health in their brand name. They also included additional health-related terms on their labels and on websites. The most commonly used were *sensitive, skin sensitivities, digestive sensitivity, digestive health, and limited/unique ingredients.*

- *Ingredients:* If you had thought there would be a handful of specific ingredients that are known to be beneficial to skin and coat, think again. The protein sources in the 24 foods were all over the map and included chicken, fish, egg, venison, beef, pork, duck, lamb, soy, peas, and turkey. A similar cornucopia was found for carbohydrate sources, with rice, potato, wheat, oats, barley, millet, corn, quinoa and tapioca all making an appearance.

- *Not so special fatty acids:* Thirteen of the 24 foods (54 %) identified fatty acids as nutrients that are important for skin and coat health. While this may be true for certain specific omega-6 and omega-3 fatty acids (and their ratios), 10 of the 13 foods did not identify these by name but instead used vague (and meaningless) terms such as "omega fatty acids" or "omega oils". Less than a third of the foods provided information about the amount of any specific fatty acid in the food. When this information was provided, the range in EPA and DHA (two important omega-3 fatty acids) concentrations overlapped with those found in foods that are *not* labeled for skin/coat health.

- *More nothin' special:* The essential nutrient content and caloric density (number of calories per cup) of the 24 foods varied enormously and overlapped with other brands that are sold for adult dogs but which are not specifically marketed for skin health. (*In other words, not to put too fine a point on it, there was nothing that was consistently special or unique about the nutrient content of these foods. Even omega-3 fatty acid concentrations were all over the map, making the claims of "Source of Omega-3 Fatty Acids" essentially useless to consumers*).

Conclusions: The researchers were rather circumspect in their conclusions, stating that the wide variety of ingredients and large range in nutritional value of products marketed for skin and coat health make product selection for owners who are interested in these foods confusing. (Personally, I go further than "confusing").

Up on My Soapbox

Up on My Soapbox: I could be wrong, but I rather doubt that a concerned owner, whose dog is experiencing skin or coat problems and who sees a food that is specifically labeled "**Sensitive Skin**", stops and ponders: "*Well, the company does not actually state outright that this food cures sensitive skin problems. Nor do they say that they have proven that the food supports healthy skin. Therefore, I know better than to expect this food to do much of anything at all to help my dog*".

I may be going out on a limb here, but I believe this owner is much more likely to be thinking "*Oh, look! A food that is designed to help Muffin's sensitive and itchy skin! I will give it a try because poor Muffin's skin has been terribly bad lately. I bet this food can help her!*" **Ka-ching.** Another day, another unregulated and misleading pet food claim, another sale. Poor Muffin.

Take Away for Dog Folks: If your dog is continually or excessively itchy or has skin problems, please make a visit to your veterinarian, not to your local pet supply store. It is important to obtain an accurate diagnosis for skin problems because the majority of these are *not related to food.* Rather, the most common causes of excessively itchiness in dogs are allergies to environmental allergens such as house dust mites, pollens and molds or fleas. Only after these causes have been eliminated should food be looked at as a potential underlying cause. (Note - The diagnosis of food allergy can only be made through the use of an 8 to 10 week elimination feeding trial, which is a topic for another time).

And, by the way, if you find Chef Michael, could you get an autograph for me?

Cited Reference: Johnson LN, Heintze CR, Linder DE, Freeman LM. Evaluation of marketing claims, ingredients, and nutrient profiles of over-the-counter diets marketed for skin and coat health of dogs. *Journal of the American Veterinary Medical Association* 2015; 246:1334-1338.

Part 2 – Smarty Pants

15
Only Have Eyes for You

*New research examines factors that may influence dogs'
inclination to follow their owner's gaze.*

Eye contact is one of the first things that I teach to my own dogs
and is a basic behavior that we teach to all of our students at my
training school, AutumnGold.

Cooper Practices Eye Contact

In our training classes, we introduce eye contact very early because it is easy to teach and provides rapid and positive results
to owners who are often frustrated with their young and exuberant dog's lack of attention. It is also a great method for teaching targeting and timing skills.

Really, what's not to like?

Well, until recently, I thought, nothing at all. However, a newly
published study motivated me to think a bit more deeply about
the behaviors that we train dogs to do and how they may, how-

ever subtlety, influence our dogs' social lives. It has to do with tests of social cognition; specifically how dogs may or may not use human gaze as a communicative signal.

Following Gaze as a Social Behavior: The inclination to follow the gaze of another individual is considered to be a socially facilitated response. It makes sense of course because one of the ways that social beings communicate is by attending to what others are paying attention to. Gaze-following behaviors have been demonstrated in a number of social species that include chimpanzees, wolves, several species of birds, domesticated goats and of course, humans. Dogs have been shown to be able to follow human gaze and other intention gestures such as pointing when engaged in an object choice test (i.e. when they are being asked to choose between a series of cups holding food). However, evidence for the dog's ability to follow a human's gaze toward distant space (i.e. when food choice is not involved) has been conflicting and inconclusive.

Why are Dogs Different from Other Social Species? Currently, there are three working theories that attempt to explain why dogs may not consistently demonstrate gaze following:

- **Habituation hypothesis:** This explanation suggests that dogs who live closely with people gradually lose their innate tendency to follow human gaze because we gaze at a lot of things that are not relevant to them. Over time, the dog will habituate to this and stop responding. (Face it, in today's world, many of us spend a lot of time staring at things that hold absolutely no interest to our dogs. Consider our use of computers, TV sets and Kindles, to name just a few).

- **Formal training hypothesis:** A second theory, and one that is not mutually exclusive of habituation (i.e. they could both be in play here), is that dogs who are formally trained to offer eye contact with their owners, either on cue or as a "default" behavior, are *less* likely to spontaneously follow the owner's gaze into space because looking into the owner's eyes is a behavior that directly competes with turning away to follow gaze. (This is the hypothesis that could put a bit of a kink in my undying love for "default eye contact" training).

- **Lifelong learning hypothesis:** A final theory that is in direct opposition to the habituation hypothesis poses that because dogs who live in homes are repeatedly asked to look to their owners for direction in many informal situations, that they actual may become *better*, not worse, at following our gaze. Examples of this are communicating to your dog that it is time for a walk (looking at the door), time to eat (gazing at the food bowl or towards the kitchen) or time for a game (searching for the favorite ball). So, in effect, the lifelong learning hypothesis works in direct opposition to the habituation hypothesis and predicts that dogs who live in homes should be quite proficient at gaze-following with their humans.

So, which of these theories (or combination) might be in play when our dogs are asked to "follow our gaze"? A group of researchers at the University of Vienna in Austria's Clever Dog Lab decided to ask a group of Border Collies.

The Study: In a cleverly designed experiment, the researchers tested all three of these hypotheses. First, they selected 147 dogs, all Border Collies living in homes as family pets. The dogs were between the ages of 6 months and 13 years. Using this wide age range allowed the researchers to test the lifelong learning and habituation hypotheses. To test the formal training hypothesis, the degree of training that each dog had received was assessed using an owner questionnaire. Dogs were classified into five categories, ranging from no formal training to extensively trained. A group of 13 additional dogs acted as a positive control group. A positive control group is subjected to a treatment [or in this case, a training procedure] that is expected to have an effect, but is not expected to have the same effect as the treatment under study. All of the dogs completed a series of three experimental phases with a familiar trainer (one of the researchers):

- **Phase 1:** In the first phase (untrained) the trainer lured the dog into position in front of her and lured or cued the dog to gaze into her eyes. As soon as the dog initiated eye contact, the trainer turned her head quickly away from the dog to gaze towards a door (test condition) or to look down at her feet (control condition).

- **Phase 2:** In the second phase, the dogs in the test group were trained to offer and hold eye contact on command. The 13 dogs in the positive control group were trained to touch a ball that was sitting on the ground with their paw. Clicker training was used to teach both behaviors.

- **Phase 3:** Following successful eye contact or touch-ball training, the dogs were retested using the techniques described in Phase 1. Instead of luring the dogs into place and to offer eye contact, the test dogs were cued to offer eye contact and the control dogs were cued to touch the ball before the trainer shifted her gaze towards the door or to her feet.

Results: Here are the researchers' findings:

- *Some dogs follow distance gaze*: In the pre-trained phase, about half of the dogs (48 %) spontaneously followed the gaze of the trainer towards the door. Although the age of the dog did not significantly influence gaze-following, young dogs in late puppyhood and geriatric dogs were more strongly inclined to look at the door than were adult, middle-aged dogs. The absence of a clear age-effect is evidence against both the habituation and the life-long learning hypotheses.

- *Training eye contact interfered with gaze following:* Following clicker training to offer eye contact, the num-

94

ber of dogs who followed the trainers gaze towards the door significantly decreased. The dogs who were trained to offer eye contact were also less likely to follow the trainer's gaze toward the door than were the dogs who had been trained to place their paw on a ball. (In other words, it was not just the training that caused the change - it was specifically training for eye contact on cue.)

- *Formal training reduced gaze following:* In both the pre-trained and the post-trained tests, dogs who had received more formal training with their owners were *less* likely to follow gaze towards the door than were dogs with little or no formal training experience. Because the dogs had a variety of training experiences, (for example obedience, agility, nose work, tricks, freestyle, search and rescue and herding), it was not possible to identify the effects of specific types of training (a subject the authors identify for future study).

- *Study limitations:* Yes, the study used just Border Collies, and yes, indeed, as a breed, they are quite the smart little peanuts. Not only are they highly trainable, but they also have a very strong tendency to look to humans for cues. The researchers acknowledge this and open up the question of what, if any, breed or breed-type differences might we expect to see in distance gaze-following behaviors? This is certainly a topic for further (if difficult to accomplish) investigation. A second issue might be the use of a door as the focus point for distance gazing. Certainly doorways are not without meaning to dogs as they are conditioned objects that predict people coming and going and opportunities for walks, which would influence a dog's tendency to respond. However, it is accepted that individuals tend to follow gaze more readily toward relevant objects. *Of interest in this study is the change in those tendencies in response to training.*

Take Away for Dog Folks: The researchers in this study were the first to show that a relatively high proportion of dogs living in homes are likely to follow a person's gaze towards distant space. In other words, they use our social cues to learn about and respond to our shared environment. Many people know this and probably will say that their dogs demonstrate this daily. However, in my view, the more important implications of these results are what they tell us about our ability to inhibit, albeit with the very best of intentions, our dog's natural social behaviors. In the study, when the same dogs were trained for a short period of time to offer eye contact on cue, the training interfered with the ability of at least some of the dogs to follow gaze. The data also showed that lifetime formal training has an inhibitory influence upon this form of social cognition in dogs.

Up on my Soapbox

Why Should We Care?

Personally, these results led me to think a bit more carefully about when and how often I ask for default eye contact with my dogs. If one agrees that social cognition, the ability to understand and respond to the social cues of others, is an important part of a dog's life quality, then we should make conscious decisions regarding the types of training that contribute to or detract from our dogs' natural social behavior.

I am certainly not advocating an end to training eye contact. For me, it remains an important behavior to teach to dogs because eye contact contributes to strong communicative bonds and facilitates learning. One cannot really teach new behaviors after all, if we fail to have our dog's attention. Rather, I am suggesting that we consciously strive for a balance between those training activities that require our dog's undivided attention and those in which we encourage dogs to use their cognitive skills and work independently.

For example, at AutumnGold we offer both Canine Freestyle and K-9 Nose Work as advanced training classes. Freestyle is tons of fun for dogs and owners and the precise training that it involves teaches body awareness, complex behaviors and chaining. Similar to obedience training, agility and many other dog sports, this training requires clear communication between trainer and dog, and eye contact is an important aspect of that communication. K-9 Nose Work on the other hand, encourages dogs to work more independently, using their scenting abilities to find a hidden object or selected scent. Like many trainers, we have found that there are very few dogs (and owners) who do not absolutely love these Nose Work games.

I am the first to say that I love having my dog's attention via eye contact, especially when we are training complex tricks, obedience exercises and Freestyle moves. However, it is every bit as exciting for me to see them work independently to find a hidden scent, play tug with their doggy friends, retrieve a hidden toy, or have free swim time in the pool. For me, these data served as a reminder that allowing our dogs to attend to their social environment, to work independently of us, and to practice (and be allowed to show) their social cognition talents are as important (and fun) as are training for good manners and canine sports.

Chippy Loves Training Nose Work!

Cited Study: Wallis LJ, Range R, Muller, CA, Serisier S, Huber L, Viranyi Z. Training for eye contact modulates gaze following in dogs. *Animal Behavior* 2015; 106:27-35.

16
With a Little Help from My Friends

Your dog's life experience and the type of training that he has had can influence whether or not he will seek your help when faced with a new task.

There is a large body of research showing that dogs are quite capable of noticing and responding to human communication cues such as body language, tone of voice, and various forms of pointing. Additionally, as we saw in the previous essay, many dogs spontaneously understand and respond to human gaze towards distant objects. There can also be a more intentional component to gaze. We all experience this when our dogs seek out and initiate eye contact with us.

Humans and dogs are well matched in this respect because humans, of course, use eye contact to communicate all of the time. Some of the reasons that we actively seek out the gaze of another person may be as a bid for attention, to communicate friendliness or animosity, or to request assistance. Similarly, many dogs will approach and initiate eye contact with their owner when they are asking for something (a walk, food, petting or a game of fetch) and in some cases, when asking for a bit of help.

These apparent requests for assistance are of interest because it seems that this is one of the ways in which dogs differ significantly from wolves. One of the earliest studies of canine social cognition compared the response of dogs and wolves when presented with an "unsolvable task" (1). In this test, the subject is first allowed to solve a food puzzle in which a bit of food in a container can be accessed by manipulating the container. After several successful trials, the nefarious researcher, unbeknownst to the dog, steps in and alters the puzzle, making the task now impossible to solve. So, the method that the dog or wolf used to previously obtain the food is now futile. (I know, frustrating. Bad researcher.)

When presented with this situation, most dogs work at the puzzle for a while and then turn to look back at their owner, presumably as a request for aid. In contrast, wolves rarely look back at humans. The initial research showing that "*wolves do not look back at humans, but dogs do*" served as the jumping-off point for a flood of innovative research regarding dogs' skills in various forms of social cognition.

Since that time, additional studies have shown that a number of factors can influence an individual dog's ability to seek and understand human gaze. Some of these are the dog's living situation (homes vs. shelters), the type of relationship that the dog has with people, and the degree and type of *training* that the dog has experienced.

Naturally, my ears perked up at this last bit - *the influence that training can have on our dogs' tendency to ask us for help.*

While still in the early stages of study, examination of the ways in which different types of training may influence a dog's inclination to "ask for help" has already provided a number of interesting results. Here are some of the major findings so far:

- *I can do it myself!* When dogs were focused on a solvable task such as learning to open a food-box with their paw or muzzle, those who had a history of formal training were *less* likely to look to their owner as they worked at the task than were dogs who had experienced little or no formal training (2). The types of training included agility, search and rescue, freestyle, hunting trials and Schutzhund, but differences between the training types were not examined.

- *Agility dogs ask; SAR dogs don't:* Conversely, when the task presented to the dogs was NOT solvable (i.e. the unsolvable task paradigm), things suddenly changed up a bit. Dogs who

100

were trained in Agility were *more* likely to look to their owners when attempting to solve the problem, while Search and Rescue (SAR) dogs were less likely (or looked for shorter durations) (3).

- ***Water rescue dogs ask (everyone):*** Another type of training that has been studied is water rescue. The training that dogs receive for this work is intensive and requires dogs to respond reliably to their handler's cues during highly stressful situations. A unique aspect is that these dogs must also be attentive to a stranger who may be behaving erratically (i.e. as he attempts to not drown). This suggests that these dogs may possess both a high degree of dependency upon their handlers' cues plus an ability to respond to a stranger and so to work somewhat independently. Indeed results of gazing tests have shown this to be true. For example, when faced with an unusual and potentially dangerous situation, water rescue dogs were more likely to look to their owners for help than were pet dogs (4). In another study, when owners and strangers were compared during the unsolvable task paradigm, water rescue dogs looked initially to their owner rather than to the stranger, but overall they gazed at both people longer than did pet dogs (5). In other words, dogs trained for water rescue preferentially looked for help from their owners, but were also willing to ask a stranger to step up and lend a hand.

With evidence showing that the specific type of work that a dog is trained to do may influence a dog's inclination to seek help from their owner (or a stranger), the same group of Italian researchers decided to look at a very specific type of training that not only requires that dogs work independently of their handlers (like SAR dogs), but in some cases, to "actively disobey", making decisions for the welfare of their sight-impaired owner.

The Study: The researchers evaluated four groups of dogs during the unsolvable task paradigm (6). These were 13 guide dogs who had just completed their training program but had not yet been placed with a blind recipient; 11 guide dogs who had been living with their blind owner for at least one year, and two pet dog control groups, one age-matched to each set of guide dogs. All of the dogs in the study were trained at the same training school and were purebred Labrador Retrievers.

Results: The researchers were interested in discovering the differences, if any, between dogs who had recently finished their guide dog training and had been housed in a kennel and those who were working as guide dogs and living with their owner and his/her family in a home. Here is what they found:

- *New guide dogs did not ask:* The recently trained dogs spent more time interacting with the apparatus and less time gazing toward the trainer or a stranger than did the older guide dogs who were living in homes (or than the pet dogs). This suggests that the recently trained dogs were more apt to work independently and less likely to "ask for help" when faced with a new and frustrating task.

- *Guide dogs in homes did ask:* In contrast, the working guide dogs who had been living in homes for at least a year were as likely to turn to look at a person to ask for help as were the pet dogs. Unlike their younger counterparts, these dogs behaved like pet dogs in that they would turn and seek help when presented with a new problem.

Was it type of training or was it living situation? There was an unavoidable confounding factor in this study. The dogs who had recently completed their training were also living in a kennel, with limited daily access to their trainer. Conversely, dogs who had been out and working for at least a year (and whose training may have lapsed to some degree) were living in homes with people, in settings similar or identical to those of pet dogs. So, the reduced tendency of the young guide dogs to seek help (and their greater inclination to work independently) may have been due to their recent training history during which many of the trained tasks required them to work independently and when they were not reinforced for giving visual attention to the trainer. Alternatively, the young dogs had also been living in a kennel and had not experienced an opportunity to develop a strong relationship with their human caretakers. Similarly, the mature guide dogs may have either experienced some lapse in training and/or may have developed a greater dependency on the humans in their home (which included both their blind handler and sighted family members).

Take-Away for Dog Folks: What these studies collectively suggest is that the life experience of training generally promotes increased confidence and independence in dogs when they are presented with novel tasks that are solvable. However, when dogs are experiencing a *failure* to succeed at a new task (and possibly are becoming frustrated), the type of training that they have experienced may influence their inclination whether or not to look to their owners for help. Dogs who have been trained to work closely with a human partner and to depend upon their cues (such as agility dogs and water rescue dogs) are more likely to look to their people for help. Conversely, dogs who have been trained at tasks in which they work more independently, such as SAR dogs and young guide dogs, are less likely to ask. Most interesting perhaps is the evidence that a dog's living situation may trump his or her training history, as seen in the guide dog study. It is possible that living in close proximity with human caretakers and experiencing daily interaction and communication may be more important than training in terms of encouraging our dogs to turn and to *ask for a little help from their friends.*

Cited Studies:

1. Miklósi A, Kubinyi E, Topál J, Gácsi M, Virányi Z, Csányi V. A Simple Reason for a Big Difference: Wolves Do Not Look Back at Humans, but Dogs Do. *Current Biology* 2003; 13:763-766.

2. Marshall-Pescini S, Valsecchi P, Petak I, Accorsi PA, Prato-Previde E. Does training make you smarter? The effects of training on dogs' performance (*Canis familiaris*) in a problem-solving task. *Behavioural Processes* 2008; 78:449-454.

3. Marshall-Pescini S, Pallalacqua C, Barnard S, Valsecchi P, Prato-Previde E. Agility and search and rescue training differently affect pet dogs' behavior in socio-cognitive task. *Behavioural Processes* 2009; 81:416-422.

4. Merola I, Marshall-Pescini S, D'Aniello B, Prato-Previde E. Social referencing: Water rescue trained dogs are less affected than pet dogs by the stranger's message. *Applied Animal Behavior Science* 2013; 147:132-138.

5. D'Aniello B, Scandurra A, Prato=Previde E, Valsecchi P. Gazing toward humans: A study on water rescue dogs using the impossible task paradigm. *Behavioural Processes* 2015: 110:68-73.

6. Scandurra A, Prato-Previde E, Valsecchi P, Aria M, D'Aniello B. Guide dogs as a model for investigating the effect of life experience and training on gazing behavior. *Animal Cognition* 2015; 18:937-944.

17
Do You Know What I Can See?

Are dogs able to consider the perspective of other they have a "theory of mind"?

Chippy, our Toller, is a terrible food thief. (Of course, the use of the word *terrible* is one of perspective. Given his impressive success rate, Chippy would argue that he is actually a very *good* food thief).

Yeah, he looks sweet.
Just don't turn your back on your toast.

Chip has become so proficient at his food thievery that our dog friends know to "keep eyes on Chippy" whenever we celebrate a birthday or have snacks after an evening of training. We are often reminded of the now infamous "*Birthday Cake Incident*" during which Chip and Grace, an equally talented Aussie friend, succeeded in reducing a section of cake to mere crumbs, no evidence to be found. Suffice it to say, we watch food in our house.

Like many other expert food thieves, Chip is quite careful in his pilfering decisions. He will only steal when we are not in the room or when we are being inattentive. The parsimonious (simplest) explanation of this is a behavioristic one; Chip learned early in life that taking forbidden tidbits was successful when a human was not in the room and was unsuccessful if someone was present and attentive to him. In other words, like many dogs who excel at food thievery, Chip learned what "works".

However, while a behavioristic explanation covers most aspects of selective stealing behavior in dogs, a set of research studies conducted by cognitive scientists suggest that there may be a bit more going on here.

Do Dogs Have a "Theory of Mind"? Dogs have demonstrated that they will alter their behavior in response to whether a person is actively gazing at them or is distracted. For example, in separate studies dogs were more apt to steal a piece of food from an inattentive person and would preferentially beg from an attentive person (1, 2). However, these differences could still be explained without a need for higher cognitive processing. A dog could learn over time that human gaze and attentiveness reliably predict certain outcomes, such as positive interactions and opportunities to beg for food. Similarly, inattentiveness might reliably predict opportunities to steal a tidbit (or two or five).

It is also possible that, just like humans, dogs use a person's gaze to determine what that individual does or does not *know*. This type of learning is considered to be a higher level of cognitive process because it requires "perspective-taking", meaning that the dog is able to view a situation through the perspective of the other individual and can then make decisions according to what they believe that he or she is aware of. The significance of this type of thinking is that it reveals at least a rudimentary "*theory of mind*" - the ability to consider what another individual knows or may be thinking.

While it has been established that dogs are sensitive to the cues that human eye contact and gaze provide (see the previous essays), it has *not* been clear whether they can use this information to determine what the person may or may not *know*.

Enter, the cognitive scientists.

The Toy Study: One approach to teasing out "*theory of mind*" evidence is to control what a dog observes about what a person may or may not be able to see. In 2009, Juliane Kaminski and her colleagues at the Max Planck institute for Evolutionary Anthropology set up a clever experiment in which they used two types of barriers; one transparent and one opaque (3). Dogs and the experimenter sat on opposite sides of the barrier, and two identical toys were placed in front of each barrier, on the same side as the dog. The dog was then asked to "Fetch!"

Results*:* They found that the dogs preferred to retrieve the toy that *both* the dog and the person could see, compared with a toy that only the dog could see. This suggests that the dogs were aware that their owners could *not know* that there was a toy located out of their view, and so retrieved the toy that they (presumably) assumed that their owner was requesting. An additional finding of this study was that the dogs were capable of this distinction only in the present, at the time that the owner's view was blocked. When the researchers tested dogs' ability to remember what the owner had been able to see in the past, such as a toy being placed in a certain location, the dogs failed at that task.

The Food Thievery Study: Recently, the same researchers provided additional evidence that dogs are able to consider what a human can or cannot see (4). A group of 28 dogs was tested regarding their tendency to obey a command to not touch a piece of food while the commanding human's ability to *see* the food was varied. The testing took place in a darkened room that included two lamps, one of which was used to illuminate the experimenter and the second to illuminate a spot on the floor where food was placed. During the test conditions, the experimenter showed a piece of food to the dog and asked the dog to "leave it" while placing the food on the ground. The experimenter alternated her gaze between the dog and the food as she gradually moved away and sat down. In two subsequent experiments using the same design, the experimenter left the room after placing the food and the degree of illumination were varied. For each experiment, four different conditions were tested: (1) Completely dark (both lamps turned off); (2) Food illuminated, experimenter dark; (3) Experimenter illuminated, food dark; (4) Food and experimenter illuminated. In all of the conditions, the dog's response with the food was recorded.

Results: There were several rather illuminating results in this study (sorry, bad pun):

- **Dogs steal in the dark (when a person is present):** When the experimenter stayed in the room, dogs were significantly more likely to steal the food when the entire room was in the dark. (They do have excellent noses, after all). If any part of the room was illuminated while the experimenter was present, the dogs were less likely to steal. Conversely, when the experimenter was *not* present, illumination made no difference at all and most of the dogs took the food. (Lights on or off; they did not care. It was time to party).

- **What the smart dog thieves do:** Within the set of dogs who *always took the food*, when the experimenter was present they grabbed the tidbit significantly faster when it was in the dark, compared to when the food was illuminated. This result suggests that the dogs were aware that the experimenter could not see the food and so changed up their game a bit. (*I'll just weasel on over to the food and snort it up.......heh heh.....she can't see it and will never know.....I am such a clever dog....*). Chippy would love these dogs.

- **It's not seeing the human.....it's what the human sees:** Collectively, the three experiments in the study showed that illumination around the *human* did not influence the dogs' behavior, while illumination around the *food* did (when a person was present). This suggests that it is not just a person's presence or attentiveness that becomes a cue whether or not to steal, but that dogs may also consider what they think we can or cannot *see* when making a decision about what to do.

Take Away for Dog Folks: Without a doubt, gaze and eye contact are highly important to dogs. They use eye contact in various forms to communicate with us and with other animals. We know that many dogs naturally follow our gaze to distant objects (i.e. as a form of pointing) and that dogs will seek our eye contact when looking for help (see *"Only Have Eyes for You"* and *"With a Little Help from My Friends"*). And now we know that dogs, like humans and several other social species, can be aware of what a person may or may not be able to see and, on some level, are capable of taking that person's perspective into consideration.

As a trainer and dog lover, I say, pretty cool stuff indeed. Chip of course, knew all of this already.

Oh, Just One More Thing......

A Caution: I was really excited about this research because these results continue to push the peanut forward regarding what we understand about our dogs' behavior, cognition, and social lives. Learning that dogs may be capable of taking the perspective of others, at least in the present, adds to the ever-growing pile of evidence showing us that our dogs' social lives are complex, rich, and vital to their welfare and life quality.

That said, because these studies had to do with dogs "behaving badly", (i.e. stealing food, Gasp! Oh No!), I was a bit hesitant to write this essay. These studies provide evidence that dogs have a lot more going on upstairs than some folks may wish to give them credit for. And as can happen with these things, evidence for one thing (*understanding that a person cannot see a bit of food and so deciding to gulp it on down*), may be inappropriately interpreted as evidence for another (*Oh! This must mean that dogs understand being "wrong"*).

Well no. It does not mean that at all.

For those who reside in the (ever diminishing) camps of "*He knows he was wrong*"; "*I trained him not to do that; He is just being willful*" and "*He must be guilty - He is showing a guilty look*": These studies show us that dogs understand what another individual may and may not know based upon what that person can see. *This is not the same, or even close to being the same, as showing that dogs understand the moral import or the "wrongness" (whatever that means) of what they choose to do.* Chippy knowing that I cannot see that piece of toast that he just pilfered is NOT the same as Chippy feeling badly that he took it. (For an in-depth look at problems with attributing guilt to dogs, see "*Death Throes of the Guilty Look*" in Part 3).

Bottom Line: These studies show us that dogs may be sneaky, but they don't say anything at all about whether they're feelin' guilty.

Cited Studies:

1. Call J, Brauer J, Kaminski J, Tomasello M. Domestic dogs (Canis familiaris) are sensitive to the attentional state of humans. *Journal of Comparative Psychology* 2003; 117:257-263.

2. Gacsi M, Miklosi A, Varga O, Topal J, Csanyi V. Are readers of our face readers of our minds? Dogs (Canis familiaris) show situation-dependent recognition of human's attention. *Animal Cognition* 2004; 7:144-153.

3. Kaminski J, Brauer J, Call J, Tomasello M. Domestic dogs are sensitive to a human's perspective. *Behaviour* 2009; 146:979-998.

4. Kaminski J, Pitsch A, Tomasello M. Dogs steal in the dark. *Animal Cognition* 2013; 16:385-394.

18
Doggie See, Doggie Do?

Does your dog learn new behaviors by watching other dogs perform them?

At my training center, AutumnGold, it is not unusual to enroll students who live with and train more than one dog. A common question that these clients have is how to arrange their training sessions to allow them to train one dog while the other dog "waits his or her turn". In most of these cases, the student laments that the dog who is not chosen for training becomes upset, does not enjoy being isolated or confined, and may even show some separation stress or frustration with the overall unfairness (in their opinion) of the entire situation.

Or, if they are clever, as my four dogs appear to be, they   apt to all participate in the training session simultaneously.

Over the years, my personal solution to this problem has been to teach each of our dogs to stay on a pause table located off of the training floor while they await their turn to train. Although it can be challenging to teach (more about this in the following essay), I like this arrangement because it is convenient and saves me from having to return to the house multiple times to get a different dog. It is also fun for the dogs because they generally receive more training time and also get to play together after the session.

Chip and Cooper wait their turns to train

It now appears that there may be additional benefits for the dogs. New research provides evidence for something that I anecdotally have observed with my own dogs and suspect that other trainers have also experienced - that dogs seem to have some ability to learn new tasks by observing other dogs. This type of learning is called *social learning* (or observational learning) and it has been studied in a variety of species and contexts. However, only recently has it been studied with dogs in a training environment.

Social Learning: It is generally accepted that social learning plays an important role in the lives of dogs. Observing the behavior of others helps dogs to learn about their environment, modifies their responses to new situations, and may even teach them new behaviors and solutions to problems. Within the broad category of social learning, several sub-classifications exist and these presumably reflect different degrees of cognitive involvement. Although there is debate among social scientists about definitions, the types include: social facilitation, local/stimulus enhancement, response facilitation, social emulation, and imitation (1).

Much of the debate among those who study social learning revolves around what information the dog is actually using and how that information is processed cognitively or consciously to change behavior. For the purposes of this essay, we are most interested in how social learning (of any type) might occur between dogs in training situations.

Interestingly, the bulk of the research that has examined social learning in dogs has focused on their ability to learn by observing *human* demonstrators. Common study paradigms ask dogs to either solve a food acquisition puzzle or to maneuver around a fence after having watched a person perform the correct solution. Dogs have been shown to be quite successful at these tasks, although factors such as the identity of the demonstrator, the dog's living situation, prior training experience and age can influence success rates.

Studies that have examined the dog's ability to learn socially from other *dogs* are fewer in number. There is evidence that, just as with human demonstrators, dogs will show improved performance and problem-solving ability after watching a demonstrator dog successfully complete a detour or puzzle task. One of earliest (and most interesting) studies reported that puppies who were allowed to observe their mother working at a scent detection task went on to become more successful as scent dogs in adult life.

Can Dogs Learn a Trained Task from Another Dog? Most recently, researchers asked whether or not learning would be enhanced in dogs who observed another dog who had been trained to perform a novel behavior (2). This study and its results have relevance to those of us who train multiple dogs and perhaps even for group training classes.

The Study: The objective of the study was to determine if learning a new task (jumping onto a trunk or small slide) was enhanced when dogs had the opportunity to observe another dog performing the exercise prior to being trained themselves. A group of 33 adult Labrador Retrievers was tested. All of the dogs were enrolled in the training program at the Italian School of Water Rescue, lived in homes with their owners, and had been pre-screened to ensure that the exercises used in the study were novel to them. The dogs were divided into two groups; an observer group and a control group. Observer dogs sat next to their owners and watched another handler and his trained demonstrator dog approach the obstacle (trunk or slide). The demonstrator dog then jumped up and sat on the obstacle. The exercise was demonstrated twice and then the observer dog and handler approached the obstacle and the handler attempted to train the dog to perform the exercise. The control group of dogs were held on lead in the same position but did not have the opportunity to watch the demonstrator dog before being trained for the new task. Each dog's success or failure to demonstrate the new behavior was recorded.

Results: The dogs who had the opportunity to observe a demonstrator dog perform the new exercises were significantly more likely to succeed at the same task when asked to perform it. Specifically, 62.5 % of the observer dogs were successful compared with 23.5 % of the control dogs. Neither a dog's sex nor his/her level of prior training experience influenced the probability that they would perform the new task successfully. Age was somewhat important, as older dogs tended to be more successful than younger dogs.

Take Away for Dog Folks: On one level, these results are not surprising. Anecdotes abound among dog folks regarding our dogs' ability to learn from one another through observation. Ask anyone who lives with more than one dog and they will relate numerous examples of their dogs sharing information (and not always in a good way). For as long as I can remember our dogs have learned to "wait" at the door and in the car by watching each other. While I do train this command, our young dogs learn to wait very rapidly when they notice that the entire family is frozen in its tracks. Similarly, because we hike a lot with our dogs, one dog finding something yummy or smelly on the trail is quickly observed and acted upon by the others. Still, these examples may arguably fall relatively low on the social learning scale as they probably reflect social facilitation or simple stimulus enhancement.

What is exciting about the recent results is that they demonstrate, albeit with a small number of dogs, that a dog who has the opportunity to observe another dog who is performing a trained exercise (and by extension, perhaps the training of that exercise itself?) can benefit from that observation. The researchers provide several possible explanations for their positive results, one of which is that dogs may show enhanced learning when they are highly motivated to engage in the task. For example, teaching something that is target-oriented, such as jumping up onto an obstacle or retrieving a toy, may be more successful than training a static exercise such as a down stay. This difference is reflected in the results of a previous study reporting that untrained dogs did *not* perform well in learning a positional behavior (lying down on command) after watching a trained dog perform it (3). While dogs are often naturally interested in examining and engaging with new objects, most are decidedly less motivated to spontaneously offer a static behavior such as a sit/stay or down/stay.

These results make me consider the relative ease with which my two youngest dogs, Ally and Cooper, have learned platform positions, retrieving tricks such as "put your toys in a basket" and go-outs to a target. Both regularly watch and get excited as the other is being trained in these behaviors. (And, not to put too fine a point on it, I rarely see that level of interest or excitement when I am training sit/stays and down/stays). While I have no control group for my own anecdotal experiences, these results suggest to me that having all of my dogs present and attending during a training session may have benefits that go beyond convenience. Watching the other dogs learn new things may help my observing dogs to learn more rapidly, at least in those exercises that interest and engage them.

And, for my clients who are attempting to train two dogs at the same time, I will now recommend that, if possible, they find a way that the dogs are able to observe each training session with the other dog. They may be very pleasantly surprised at the results.

Cited References:

1. Kubinyi E, Pongracz P, Miklosi A. Dog as a model for studying conspecific and heterospecific social learning. *Journal of Veterinary Behavior* 2009; 4:31-41.

2. Scandurra A, Mongillo P, Marinelli L, Aria M, D'Aniello B. Conspecific observational learning by adult dogs in a training context. *Applied Animal Behaviour Science* 2016; 174:116-120.

3. Tennie C, Glabsch E, Tempelmann S, Brauer J, Kaminski J, Call J. Dogs, *Canis familiaris*, fail to copy intransitive actions in third-party contextual imitation tasks. *Animal Behavior* 2009; 77:1491-1499.

19
Manners Minder and Me

Do remote training devices enhance learning or lead to "device obsession"?

In the previous essay, "*Doggie See, Doggie Do?*" I discussed research showing that dogs may be capable of learning new tasks simply by observing another dog being trained. I mentioned that when I work with my own dogs, I rotate among them by training each dog to perform a down/stay on the pause tables located on the side of our training floor.

Chip and Cooper Wait Their Turns to Train

In our family, Chippy and Cooper are the most recent in a long line of Case dogs who have learned to "wait their turn" on their platform bed. Admittedly, this is not an easy behavior to teach seeing that my dogs love to train and ultimately view their time on the platform as the "*down-stays of doom*".

The approach to training this is pretty simple. I first teach a solid down-stay on the platform with no distractions, and then shape time and distance separately using click/treat. Getting a solid down stay on the platform is the easy part......the difficulty lies in getting that stay to hold while another dog is out on the floor, having all of the fun. Until recently, I accomplished this by returning to the platform frequently with a click/treat for staying, gradually lengthening the time interval between each reinforcement (+R). If the dog frequently jumped off of the platform, I would lower my criteria or put the dog in the x-pen and return to the task at another time.

Enter Alice (aka Alice Bo-Balice), our newest family member.

With Ally, I decided to change things up a bit and use a remote training device for this task. There are several commercial versions of these available, and I used a "Manners Minder" (now called "Treat & Train"). This device was initially created by the late Dr. Sophia Yin and it functions by providing remote +R in the form of small dry or semi-moist treats. Delivery can be controlled either manually with a handheld control or via an automatic and adjustable reinforcement program. A tone precedes treat delivery and is used as a conditioned reinforcer.

The Questions: I know that I can teach this behavior to Ally using the same +R approach that I have used in the past with our other dogs. However, I wondered whether training a down/stay on a platform might be more efficient using a remote trainer. As I see it, there could be both benefits and potential disadvantages to these devices:

Potential Advantages:

- The remote trainer is a large and physically obvious cue that can be paired with the target area (bed) and which becomes a conditioned reinforcer (i.e. its presence consistently predicts the arrival of a primary reinforcer in the form of treats). This is an advantage in that it quickly signaled to Ally that the bed was "the place to be" whenever the Manners Minder was placed there.

- It provides +R remotely that is associated with a particular target (bed) and is disassociated from the trainer (me). [Note: I consider this property both an advantage and a disadvantage - see below].

- It allows the use of a very precise intermittent reinforcement schedule (I used variable intervals, called the "down stay" setting with the device, but there are several available settings).

Potential disadvantages:

- The trained behavior may become dependent on the presence of the device. I suspect that Ally's down stay may, at least initially, break down when I attempt to remove the device and +R her down/stay in its absence.

- The device may malfunction. This happens relatively frequently, when treats get stuck in the mechanism, leading to poor timing and frustration for the dog.

- It provides +R that is disassociated from the trainer. One of the best things about training dogs, in my view, is that it enhances communication with our dogs and strengthens the bonds that we have with them. Removing the trainer (me) from this equation therefore removes a number of opportunities for positive interaction and bond-building with Ally.

What does the Science say? To date, there are two published studies of the effectiveness of remote training devices for teaching targeted down/stays with dogs. The first of these was conducted by Dr. Sophia Yin and published in 2008 and the second, using a similar device, was conducted by a group of researchers from Budapest, Hungary in 2016 (1, 2). Let's see what they have to say:

Study 1: This study was conducted in two phases, each using dogs who had a history of problem behaviors at the door (rushing, barking). In the first phase, six dogs were trained by an experienced dog trainer in a laboratory setting to move to a platform bed and offer a down stay using the Manners Minder. In the second phase, the same training protocol was used with a group of 15 dogs who were trained in their homes by their owner. A control group of 6 dogs received no training at all.

Results: All six dogs who were trained in the laboratory setting successfully learned to maintain a down stay on a bed for a period of 1 minute, when trained using the remote trainer. In phase 2, although the average amount of training time was longer, all of the owners successfully trained their dogs to complete a down stay on a targeted bed when visitors came to the door. The owners also reported significant decreases in problem behaviors associated with greeting at the door. (*Note: The study protocol did not include removing the device from the targeted bed*).

Study 2: The researchers in this study asked whether dissociating the trainer from the +R by using a remote delivery device would influence dogs' responses to a known command. The study design manipulated how +R was delivered to dogs while owners asked their dogs to "sit" and to "down". One group of owners directly reinforced their dog with a food treat while the second group reinforced using a remote delivery device that was located next to the dog. After the practice session, the dog's response to the owner's commands was measured with the owner either standing next to the dog, 10 feet away, or hidden behind a screen.

Results: All of the dog responded well to both types of positive reinforcement. The performance rate during the test phase (no +R given) was similar for the two groups when the handler was standing close. However, when the owner moved away or was out of sight, dogs who had been reinforced with the remote device performed better than dogs who had been reinforced directly by their owner. Performance declined in both groups, but it declined *less* in the group that had been reinforced with the device. An important note is that while the handler moved away from the dogs, *the device did not.* Rather, it remained where it had been during training, immediately next to the dog. (This is equivalent to the device remaining on the bed or platform in targeted training). Therefore, a significant difference between the two groups was that the "opportunity for reinforcement" as represented by the device itself was still very much in evidence to dogs who had been previously trained with it, but the handler was not. (*One is left to wonder again, what would be the results if the device had been moved as well?*).

Ally's Training: So, here is where we are with our little gal's training. Ally has rapidly learned to offer a down/stay on her pause table when the Manners Minder is present. She can maintain a down/stay for 10 minutes or more when I am training another dog, using a relatively "thin" intermittent and variable interval +R schedule programmed on the device (30 seconds or more). The caveat is that she is successful with this provided the training that I am doing with the other dog is not something that is highly motivating to her, such as retrieving or Nosework. Conversely, when training those activities with Cooper or Chippy, I reduce the schedule to ~ 10 seconds and she can (usually) maintain her stay. Since Ally is just 10 months old, is a very high energy field Golden, and literally lives to retrieve, I consider this to be a great success and would say that at this level, I am very pleased with her progress and with the Manners Minder approach.

Next Steps: My goal with Ally is the same as with my other dogs - to have a reliable down stay on the pause table while she is not currently being trained. Because I interchange dogs often during training sessions, I would like to remove the device altogether and have a solid stay that is "*Manners Minder-Free*". To accomplish this, I must shift Ally's focus for her +R away from the device and back to me (the source of click/treat). I am gradually reducing the frequency of +R from the device by increasing its interval, and then stepping in to +R in the breaks.

Positively reinforcing Ally's down stay with click/treat

The results of the 2016 study predict that Ally may have some reduction in response when I move further away from her. However, it also predicts that keeping the device present will mitigate those mistakes. Therefore the big question continues to be one that the research has not yet addressed: "*What will happen if/when I remove the device itself?*"

Bye-Bye Manners Minder: Some trainers who use these devices solve this issue by not having it in the first place - *they don't remove the device.* They keep it on the dog's bed or other targeted area and simply modify the intermittent schedule of +R that it delivers. Okay, well, call me a purist, but I would like to teach Ally to offer a solid down/stay without an enormous cue sitting there like a new-age, belching, vending machine. Maybe I want my cake and to eat it too....but, like her brothers, I would like Ally to have the opportunity to watch training and get some of those demonstrated observational learning benefits that we recently learned about.

And, here it comes......there is something *else* that has been niggling at me about this device.........

Up On My Box Again

Down Stay or Obsession? I have noticed a clear difference between training Ally to stay using the Manners Minder and my experiences training my other dogs using a more traditional click/treat approach. First, before Device Lovers out there start sputtering and spamming, I totally get that this device works. It actually works almost too well. Ally is less than a year old and I have a steady, if rather frenetic, platform stay with her. However, I have to question whether this stay reflects Ally having an understanding of "*I maintain a down stay on my table until it is my turn to train*" versus a more insidious reflection of; "*I am obsessed with this little machine that occasionally and somewhat unpredictably burps out a treat at me*".

There are definitely signs of the latter. When Ally sees the device, she gets excited and immediately books it for the pause table. When it beeps, she fixates on the tray with an intensity that borders on that of, well, an addict (hello dopamine). The tiny little

125

treat arrives and she is back at it, staring, staring, hoping to hear that next beep.

We all know that look. (Consider any present-day teen, walking along the street, staring down at his or her cell phone).

In addition to these signs of device obsession, Ally also shows varying degrees of frustration. She becomes conflicted between staring at the device (a look I am starting to loathe) and watching one of her brothers engage in something fun on the training floor. Certainly, my dogs all show some frustration (barking, excitement) when they observe another dog retrieving or finding a scent at Nosework. But this is different in some crucial way because Ally rapidly and frantically vacillates between staring at the device and trying to keep up with what is going on around her.

Bottom Line: My opinion and these experiences are not meant to disparage the use of remote food dispensing devices in dog training. I value the rapid response that Ally has shown to using the Manners Minder to train her pause table stay. However, I do worry about the obsessive nature of her response and I question how things will go when we begin to remove the dispenser from the table. I also wonder if what appears to be a down stay when we describe it using observable behaviors may in actuality be something else - an obsession with a technology and the absence of learning. Whether this intense focus is something that I can segue into a device-free down stay that is reinforced and maintained with click/treat with Ally remains to be seen. It also remains to be studied or reported in the research, something that I hope will be remedied in the near future!

Cited Studies:

1. Yin S, Fernandez EJ, Pagan S, Richardson SL, Snyder G. Efficacy of a remote-controlled, positive-reinforcement, dog training system for modifying problem behaviors exhibited when

people arrive at the door. *Applied Animal Behaviour Science* 2008; 113:123-138.

2. Gerencser L, Kosztolanyi A, Delanoeije J, Mikosii A. The effect of reward-handler dissociation on dogs' obedience performance in different conditions. *Applied Animal Behaviour Science* 2016; 174:103-110.

20
The Meaning of Click

Is the sound of click a secondary reinforcer, a marker, a bridging stimulus, or all three?

Hi. My name is Linda and I am a clicker trainer. In the spirit of full disclosure, I admit that I have been using a clicker for many years. My use began with the common gateway secondary reinforcer, the verbal cue ("Yes!"). While that worked well for a while, I eventually found that I needed more. I wanted a marker that was accurate and clear to my dog and something that could provide that immediate "ah ha!" moment in dog training that we all crave.

Recently, my husband suggested that perhaps I am too dependent upon my clicker. It is possible that finding them all over the house, in the pockets of my jackets and jeans, in the car, and oh yeah, one in the refrigerator, had something to do with his concern. I emphatically denied this and insisted that I could quit clicker training any time that I wanted to.

He called my bluff and suggested that I try using food alone, no clicker. Admittedly, I did not react well.

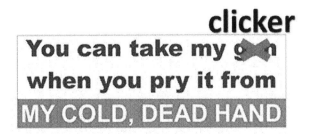

Hyperbole aside, why is it that many trainers, myself included, are so completely sold on clicker training? While the short answer is a forehead thumping "*Duh.....because it works so well*", a longer exploration into clicker training, plus a bit of science, is needed to fully understand this phenomenon.

Operant Learning: There is a large body of scientific evidence supporting the effectiveness of using consequences to teach new behaviors, a type of associative learning called operant learning or conditioning. Although the consequences that are used can be either aversive or pleasurable, most trainers focus on pleasurable consequences, or positive reinforcers. For dogs, a universal primary positive reinforcer is food, though verbal praise, petting, and play are also important. (Note: A primary reinforcer is a stimulus that is inherently rewarding to the animal, with no need for prior conditioning). Animals learn most efficiently when the targeted behavior is immediately followed by delivery of the positive reinforcer. Even brief delays between the behavior and the reinforcer can slow or prevent learning.

The Timing Issue: Herein lies the problem. In the practical context of animal training, there are numerous situations in which it is impossible for a trainer to deliver a primary reinforcer at the exact time that the desired behavior is being offered. Examples with dogs include when teaching retrieving, targeting distant objects, or moving a paw or other body part in a very precise manner. Secondary reinforcers help to solve this problem. These are signals that are clear to the animal, such as a sound or light flash, and which are purposefully paired with a primary reinforcer. For marine mammal trainers, a whistle is used. For dog trainers, it is the click.

Click-Treat: The sound of the clicker is transformed from a neutral (meaningless) stimulus to a conditioned (secondary) stimulus by repeatedly pairing the click sound with the delivery of a food treat (the primary reinforcer). After multiple repetitions of Click-Treat (hereafter CT), in which the click sound reliably precedes and predicts the treat, the click begins to possess the same properties as the treat itself. Clicker training allows the trainer to precisely target (mark) tiny bits of behavior at the exact moment they are occurring. The click sound becomes analogous to a bridge in time - saying to the dog *"That's it!! That thing that you are doing right this instant is what will earn you the yummy treat that is coming shortly!"*

Well, at least that is what we *think* the click means to our dogs.........

The Meaning of Click: Recently, a team of Australian researchers reviewed clicker training and examined the mechanisms through which clicker training might enhance learning (1). They looked at each of the three functions that dog trainers typically attribute to the click - a secondary reinforcer, a marker of behavior, and as a bridging stimulus. Although we typically give equal weight to all three of these functions, the current evidence, collected primarily in laboratory animals and pigeons, is telling us differently:

Secondary Reinforcer? As described earlier, once a clicker is "charged" as a secondary reinforcer, it should possess the same reinforcing properties as the primary reinforcer (treat). This means that the click sound alone, without being followed by a treat, is expected to cause an increase in the targeted behavior and help learned behaviors to be resistant to extinction. An unpairing of the connection between secondary and primary reinforce should also lead to a lessening of these effects. All of these outcomes have been tested in rats and pigeons and the evidence overwhelmingly suggests that a conditioned signal (click), when consistently paired with a primary reinforce (treat) does indeed take on the properties of the primary reinforcer.

The researchers also provide evidence (in rats) of a neuropsychological nature - dopamine release has been shown to occur at times that would be expected if a secondary reinforcer was the driving mechanism for learning.

Event Marker? Almost all clicker trainers, when asked to explain why clicker training works so well, include some version of *"it precisely marks the behavior that I wish to reinforce, at the exact moment that it is happening"*. I agree with this account, given my own practical training experiences. But, of course, belief is not the same as evidence. What does the current science say about using an auditory signal to mark behavior? As a marker, the signal (click) must draw the animal's attention to the event. So, if a signal functions to mark behavior, we would expect to see an effect of the signal, though at a lower intensity, when it is not paired with a primary reinforcer. For dogs, this means that hearing the "click" sound, regardless of its pairing with food, should emphasize that moment and thus enhance learning whatever behavior is occurring. Again, though not tested with dogs (yet), this hypothesis has been tested with laboratory animals. The evidence suggests that learning is *somewhat* enhanced by a marker alone but that the pairing of the marker with a primary reinforcer is decidedly more potent. While "click" may indeed be a marker for behaviors, this function is intricately related to its role as a secondary reinforcer rather than marking an event simply by bringing the animal's attention to it.

Bridging Stimulus? The bridging stimulus hypothesis focuses on the *"a treat will be coming to you soon"* portion of clicker training. This function applies when the dog is a distance away from the trainer or there is a temporal (time) delay between the behavior and delivery of the food treat. According to the bridging hypothesis, rather than simply marking the behavior, the signal communicates to the animal that reinforcement will be delayed (but is still promised). A limited number of published studies have examined this function, but the evidence that is available suggests that an auditory signal (such as a click) *may* bridge the temporal gap between behavior and food. However, all of the studies used a type of training process called "autoshaping" which is a highly controlled and contrived experimental process. Whether or not a click acts as a bridge in the practical and varied setting of dog training remains to be studied.

Take Away for Dog Folks: The bulk of the current evidence coming from other species, primarily lab animals who are tested in highly controlled conditions, tells us that the major way in which clicker training enhances learning is through the click's function as a secondary reinforcer. As far as event marking and acting as a bridging stimulus, these may be in effect, but if so, they are in a supporting role rather than being the star players.

So what might this information mean for we who love to click?

1. In its role as a secondary reinforcer, the click takes on the pleasurable properties of the primary reinforcer, food treats. Pairing of the click with the treat (charging the clicker) is essential to both establish and maintain these properties.

2. While clicking *without* treating will work for a short period of time, repeated uncoupling of the click from the treat will eventually extinguish the connection and the click will stop being effective as it gradually reverts to a neutral stimulus.

3. Although most of us refer to the click as "marking" behaviors, the actual marking properties of the click appear to be intricately linked to its function as a secondary reinforcer, rather than having any stand-alone strength in this capacity. Ditto for bridging stimulus.

Bottom line? Given these three suppositions, if you are a trainer and are in the habit of regularly clicking without treating, you may want to stop doing that (2). The power of the click lies principally in its strength as a secondary (conditioned) reinforce, so maintaining that connection appears to be key.

As for me, this evidence provides further support for the strength of clicker training with dogs. Don't think I will be going through any 12-step program to reduce my dependency anytime soon.

Cited Papers:

1. Feng LC, Howell TJ, Bennett PC. How clicker training works: Comparing reinforcing, marking, and bridging hypotheses. *Applied Animal Behaviour Science* 2016; Accepted paper, in press.

2. Martin S, Friedman SG. Blazing clickers. *Paper presented at Animal Behavior Management Alliance Conference,* Denver, CO, 2011.

21
Just Show Me a Sign

Do dogs have a preference of verbal versus gestural (hand signal) cues? New research asks a group of trained water rescue dogs to tell us.

Like many dog trainers, I use both verbal and gestural (hand) signals as cues with my dogs. With students at AutumnGold, we introduce both verbal and physical cues at the same time, but generally emphasize verbal signals because this is what most pet owners prefer to use with their dogs.

All of our classes include instructions for fading gestural cues in favor of verbal cues for owners who wish to use primarily verbal signals. Students are taught to "*lead with the verbal cue and follow with the gesture*", thus establishing a classical relationship (verbal signal predicts gesture signal). This connection allows the trainer to gradually fade the hand signal and eventually to rely primarily on the verbal command.

On the other hand (literally), hand signals are a lot of fun to teach and come in "handy" in a wide variety of exercises. For these, we offer a dedicated "hand signals" class, for students who are interested in teaching their dog distance signals and gesture cues for direction or jumping. This is great fun for dogs and their people and is also helpful for students who are interested in competing in dog sports.

However, like many dog training practices, the use of verbal versus hand signals with dogs has not been formally studied. Until recently, that is.

Enter Biagio D'Aniello and his team of scientists at the University of Naples (among others) in Italy. I have written about this group's research on previous occasions. They work with retrievers who are trained for water rescue work and are reporting new information regarding the dog's communication skills and ability to learn through observation (see the previous essays "*With a Little Help from My Friends*" and "*Doggie See, Doggie Do*").

This time around, the researchers asked whether dogs who are trained to respond equally to verbal and gestural cues show a preference for one type over the other.

The Study: A group of 25 certified water rescue dogs were enrolled. The group included 10 Golden Retrievers and 15 Labrador Retrievers, composed of 12 males and 13 females. Per training protocols for water rescue, all of the dogs had been trained to respond to both verbal and gestural cues. The dogs were tested in four behaviors; sit, down, stay and come. The study was conducted in three phases. *Phase 1:* The four basic commands were given using gestures only. *Phase 2:* Commands were delivered using a verbal cue only. *Phase 3:* (Here is where things get tricky). Both forms of a command were given, but *incongruently* (i.e. they conflicted with each other). For example, the verbal command for "sit" was paired with the gesture for "down", the verbal command for "come" was paired with the gesture for "stay", etc. The frequencies of correct responses were recorded in the first two phases, and a "preference index" that indicated the percent of correct gestural responses was calculated for the third phase.

Results:

1. **Just a sign, please:** When gestures alone were used, all of the dogs responded correctly to all four commands, with the exception of a single error (one dog missed a "down" signal). In contrast, when verbal cues were used, the dogs made a total

of *18 errors*. The most common mistake was failing to lie down in response to the verbal command "down". These results suggest that dogs who were trained using both verbal and hand signal cues (and when no attempt was made to emphasize one type of signal over the other), the dogs responded more consistently to gestures than to verbal cues.

2. **Location, location, location:** While dogs showed an overall preference for gestures over verbal commands, this preference was not found when the verbal command to "come" was paired with the hand signal "stay" and the owner was located a distance away from the dog. In this case, the majority of dogs (56 %) responded to the verbal command. This difference suggests that although the dogs tended to pay more attention to hand signals than to verbal commands, this preference may be overridden by a desire to stay in close proximity to the owner.

3. **Girls may be more visual:** An interesting result of this paper was the sex difference that was found. Female dogs showed a strong preference for responding to hand gesture cues, while males were more likely to respond equally to both types of cue. (Note: Although there is a bit of previous research suggesting that female dogs concentrate more on visual cues than do males, the small numbers in this trial coupled with the method of scoring that was used lead the researchers to interpret this result with caution - in other words, this may be a "statistical hiccup").

This pilot study suggests that when dogs are trained to both hand signals and verbal commands, they will respond most consistently to hand signals. The study also suggests that context is an important factor, in that having a preference to be close to the trainer may override the tendency to focus on gestural signals, leading a dog to choose the signal (verbal or gestural) that leads to proximity.

Take Away for Dog Folks: The finding that dogs (usually) respond better to hand signals than they do to verbal cues is probably not surprising to most trainers. This certainly supports our understanding of dogs as being highly responsive to body language and non-verbal cues. Still, it is always gratifying to find scientific data that supports one's (previously unsupported) suppositions.

Do hand signals have *enhanced* saliency? However, is it possible that there is more to the differences found in this study than is explained by the dog's proclivity for reading body language? This research lead me to think more deeply about these two types of signals; specifically about the type of gestural signals that we choose to use. The majority of hand signals that we use in dog training are far from being arbitrary signals. Rather they are structured in both form and function to direct the dog's attention or body to the targeted behavior.

For example, a commonly used hand signal for "down" is a sweeping motion from the dog's "nose to his toes". During training, this gesture easily doubles as both a lure when food is held in the hand and as a vehicle to deliver positive reinforcement when the hand delivers a food treat once the dog attains the down position. A reliable response to the hand signal alone is achieved by gradually removing the lure from the signaling hand and switching to +R from the opposite hand. We are then left with a hand signal that has, well, *enhanced saliency* for the dog, if you will. A second example is the use of body language and hand signals to inform a dog about the direction to run or jump in agility training. The physical signal itself has inherent meaning to the dog (we all get this). This signal is then enhanced by pairing it with food or an opportunity to tug.

Contrast these gesture examples to the variety of verbal cues that we use with dogs (sit, down, come, etc.). All of these, of course, are completely arbitrary from the dog's point of view. We could just as easily use the word "down" to train a lie down command as the word "pumpkin" or "fluffy butt". While we do enhance saliency by pairing these terms with reinforcers, they cannot be structured in the same way that gestures can to be naturally obvious (salient) to the dog.

So, in addition to dogs being highly attentive to body language (I think we all agree on that), it also seems that the hand signals that we select function to naturally attract our dog's attention and to direct behavior. The trainer "beefs up" this attraction by pairing the signal with positive reinforcement. Therefore, gestural cues may always have one step up over verbal cues when comparing the two (when the owner is in close proximity). Here is an idea - try training a sit using a down hand signal or teaching an agility dog to jump in the *opposite* direction from which you are pointing. In addition to this being a bit of a training challenge (more than a bit, I suspect), I would hypothesize that when arbitrary gestural signals are compared with verbal cues, we might see a leveling out of the preferences for gesture versus verbal signals.

A role for individual preference and reinforcement history?
I also pondered what the influence of an *individual's* preference might be in this type of testing. All dogs tend to have certain exercises that they enjoy more than others. Some of these exercises may be inherently reinforcing for the dog while others may simply be preferred because they have a strong reinforcement history with the trainer (i.e. the exercise has been practiced and reinforced more frequently). In the case of this study, we might expect that dogs trained for water rescue work would be highly bonded to their owners and would also have a very strong reinforcement history for the "come" command. It would be interesting to explore verbal versus gesture preferences in dogs who are trained for different types of work, who may have different behavior preferences and reinforcement histories. Such a test would be analogous to the study that this same group of researchers did with dog's looking back for help, in which they found some very interesting differences.

138

In practice: From a practical viewpoint, as a trainer, these results suggest to me that we should be doubly careful when fading hand signals in favor of verbal cues, especially when training a dog's less preferred behaviors. While this research suggests that dogs are asking us to "just show me a sign", it also seems that their responses will be influenced by a number of factors, including looking for the cue that tells them what they want to hear!

Cited Study: D'Aniello B, Scandurra A, Alterisio A, Valsecchi P, Prato-Previde E. The importance of gestural communication: A study of human-dog communication using incongruent information. *Animal Cognition 2016; DOI:* 10.1007/s10071-016-1010-5.

22
The Inhibited Dog (It's not what you think)

New research examines how a dog's personality and state of arousal influence problem-solving ability.

We recently started a new Beginner class at AutumnGold, a course designed for dogs who have had little or no previous training. Generally this class is composed of young dogs less than one year of age and a few older dogs who have been recently adopted from a shelter or rescue group. We host a 90-minute orientation on the first evening for owners only. The orientation introduces students to our training principles, provides guidelines for keeping dogs safe and comfortable in a group setting, and prepares owners for what to expect the following week when they arrive with their dogs.

This preparation is absolutely necessary because unbeknownst to the owners, their dogs will be arriving at class ready to party down. New place, other dogs (who are also excited), lots of great doggy smells, toys, and treats (lots of treats). From a dog's point of view; definitely a time for celebration.

Knowing that the energy level in the training hall will be tipping the high end of the scale on the first night (and probably on several thereafter), we emphasize to students that the one hour or so that they spend at class each week is primarily for them to learn how to train their dogs and for their dogs to have an evening out for some socialization and fun. We stress that because the dogs will be excited and distracted, they generally learn very little during class time. Rather, dogs will do most of their learning at home during daily training sessions, when they are less excited and stimulated (an emotional state that is often technically referred to as "arousal").

While trainers who teach group classes are anecdotally aware of the impact that excitability can have on a dog's ability to learn, it is only recently that the specific effects of arousal on dogs' cognitive ability has been studied by researchers. This work is highly relevant to trainers because understanding more about the contextual nature of how dogs learn can help us to more effectively structure our classes, inform our clients and train our own dogs.

The Science: The story begins with the concept of "*inhibitory control*", a term that refers to an individual's ability to resist the impulse to do something that may be immediately gratifying but is ultimately harmful or counterproductive. (Though not technically correct, dog trainers often colloquially refer to this as "impulse control"). Examples in dog training abound. A dog who correctly responds to a "leave it" command and turns away from the smelly thing on the ground is demonstrating excellent inhibitory control. So is the dog who maintains her sit/stay while the cat wanders past or waits patiently at the open door prior to going for a walk. While we certainly capitalize on our dog's ability to use this talent and hone it carefully with training, many exercises that allow our dogs to live with us as well-mannered family members would not be possible if dogs did not possess an innate capacity for inhibitory control when learning new tasks.

Inhibitory control has been studied in many species, including our own. A body of evidence in humans suggests that an individual's ability to forego instant gratification in lieu of a more nuanced and considered response is relatively stable over time and across contexts. In other words, some people demonstrate high degrees of inhibitory control in many areas of their lives. Other people, not so much.

What about Dogs? The same may be true for dogs. Recent evidence suggests that the type of work that a dog has been selected for can influence the strength of a dog's capacity for inhibitory control. For example, a successful herding dog has a strong chase drive yet inhibits the final bite portion of predatory drive. Simi-

141

larly, dogs selected for Service Dog or Search and Rescue work must maintain concentration and continue to work in the face of situations that are highly variable and distracting.

However, personality (temperament) alone does not fully explain a dog's capacity for inhibitory control.

Not Just a Personality Trait: The expression of inhibitory control can also be influenced by a variety of situational or environmental factors. One of the most important of these is an individual's current state of emotional arousal (think - the excited beginner dog). The emotional-reactivity hypothesis explains this in terms of arousal's ability to either *support* or *interfere* with learning and performance. It is a bit of a "Three Bears" scenario in which too little arousal is not a good thing (the individual is not interested or is not attending to the task), while neither is too high a state of arousal (the individual is highly distracted and excitable). The "just right" level exists somewhere in the middle - a moderate state of emotional arousal that best supports an individual's ability to demonstrate inhibitory control and learn new tasks.

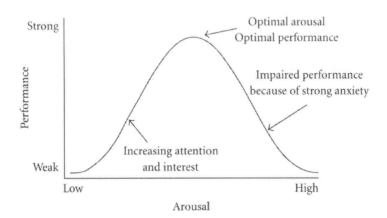

Optimal Inhibitory Control (Performance) Occurs at Moderate Levels of Emotional Arousal

It appears that a dog's ability to demonstrate inhibitory control may be influenced by both personality traits (temperament) and the dog's current state of emotional arousal. This information is certainly not surprising to anyone who trains dogs. However, the interesting part has to do with new research suggesting that emotional arousal can have *different* effects upon learning in dogs, depending upon a dog's innate personality.

The Study: Emily Bray and her colleagues at the Duke Canine Cognition Center theorized that dogs selected for different types of work might differ in their natural state of emotional arousal and that changing their arousal state might either enhance or inhibit learning - as expressed as inhibitory control. Specifically, they noted that Labrador Retrievers who have been selected and bred to work as Service Dogs (assistance dogs) undergo intentional breeding selection for low levels of emotional arousal and high trainability. Conversely, the absence of such selective breeding pressures on pet dogs suggests that, as a group, Labrador Retrievers who have been acquired as pets would be more emotionally reactive and thus more innately (and easily) aroused by comparison.

Given the inverted U-shaped curve for performance, they predicted that assistance dogs, having a more placid temperament by nature, would demonstrate their best inhibitory control when purposefully aroused (to move them from the left tail of the curve to the right a bit), while pet dogs would benefit from a bit of calming experience to move them from the overly aroused tail on the right side of the curve, toward the left. Put another way; they expected pet dogs to be more prone to errors in inhibitory control due to over-arousal and assistance dogs to be more prone to errors caused by under-arousal.

They tested this in a group of 30 pet dogs and a group of 76 Labrador Retrievers who had been bred as potential assistance dogs by Canine Companions for Independence. A standard fence detour task was used to measure problem-solving ability (performance). This tasks requires that dogs demonstrate inhibitory control because while they can see a dog treat behind the apex of a transparent barrier, solving the problem requires the dog to move away from the treat and walk around the end of the barrier in order to access the reward.

Each dog was tested in two states of emotional arousal; low and high. In the low arousal condition, the experimenter encouraged the dog to complete the detour task using a calm and quiet voice. In the high arousal condition, the experimenter encouraged the dog using a high-pitched and excited voice. Dogs' success and ability to show inhibitory control was measured according to the pathway that they attempted to travel, whether or not they tried to grab the treat directly (through the barrier) and the amount of time that it took the dog to succeed.

Results: Statistically significant differences were found between the pet dogs and the assistance dogs and between low and high emotional arousal states. Here is what the researchers discovered:

- **Pet dogs are more excitable:** As a group, the pet dogs had a higher baseline level of emotional arousal (excitability) when compared with the assistance dogs. This result was expected and supported the supposition that assistance dogs are selected for emotional stability and calm temperaments while many pet dogs, well, are not.

- **Assistance dogs performed best when emotionally aroused:** During the detour tasks, the assistance dogs performed significantly better (i.e. exerted more inhibitory control) when they were aroused emotionally by the excited experimenter, compared with when they were calmed by the quiet experimenter. In other words, excitable encouragement and a high-pitched voice *improved* these dogs' ability to problem solve and to show inhibitory control.

144

- **Pet dogs performed best when calmed:** The exact opposite was true for pet dogs. Pet dogs achieved significantly better detour success scores when encouraged in a calming and monotone voice (low emotional arousal) compared with when they were encouraged to succeed using highly arousing encouragement. Therefore, encouraging pet dogs in a highly excitable manner *interfered with learning, reduced inhibitory control, and lessened success.*

Take Away for Dog Folks: This information should be of great interest to anyone who trains dogs and in particular to those of us who teach group classes - situations that, by definition, lead to high states of emotional arousal in the majority of dogs. While most trainers intuitively know that a highly aroused (excited) dog does not learn efficiently, these data show us that a specific type of problem-solving, inhibitory control, will be impaired in pet dogs who are over-stimulated. Therefore when training an excited dog to maintain a sit/stay, to "leave it" or to "wait" at the door, we will do best to use a calming voice, quiet demeanor, and to manage the dog's environment (as much as is possible) to ratchet down emotional arousal. Similarly, an older, calm dog who perhaps has "seen it all" and is participating in an advanced training class, may benefit from exercises that *enhance,* rather than suppress, emotional arousal. Hence the adage - *Active praise for action exercises.*

The Bottom Line? Knowing where that sweet spot is on the inverted U-curve for an individual dog in a given situation may have as much to do with who that dog is in terms of his natural state of arousal as it does with manipulating the training environment to increase or decrease that state. An appropriately "inhibited" dog, one whose cognitive faculty of inhibitory control is functioning at its best, may be the dog who is moderately but not excessively emotionally aroused.

Cited Study: Bray EE, MacLean EL, Hare BA. Increasing arousal enhances inhibitory control in calm but not excitable dogs. *Animal Cognition* 2015; 18:1317-1329.

23
I Bow for Your Play

What is your dog communicating to other dogs when he offers a play bow? New research has some answers.

At AutumnGold we have an informal group of trainers and dog friends who get together regularly to do a bit of dog training, go for group walks, and give our dogs free time to play. During play time, we take care that the dogs who are loose together know one another well, are comfortable together and demonstrate good play manners. We include plenty of "calling out of play" and play pauses to keep things safe and tension free. One of the most enjoyable things about these sessions is that they give us a chance to watch our dogs having fun together and to observe the many ways in which dogs communicate during play.

The Science: While many of us learn a great deal from watching our dogs play, there is also a substantial body of science on this topic. Researchers have long been interested in the expression and functions of animal play in a variety of species. Specific studies of play in dogs are not as numerous, but several scientists, such as Marc Bekoff, Nicola Rooney, John Bradshaw and Alexandra Horowitz have published work that examines play behavior in young and adult dogs.

Most recently, a team of researchers at the University of Michigan focused their work on a very specific component of canine play (1).

The Play Bow

The play bow is a common and highly stereotyped play signal in dogs (and several other canid species as well). However, the precise meaning of this posture is not completely understood. Marc Bekoff's earlier work with puppies and young adults suggested that dogs tend to bow prior to making a move that might be misconstrued by their play partner, such as feigning a bite or attack, as a way to clarify playful intent (2). In other words, the play bow is analogous to a dog saying *"Hey, dude. Just wanted to remind you that this is all play. I just mention this because the next thing that I plan to do is well.....bite your ear. Remember this is all play, 'kay?"*

Other possible functions of play bows are as visual signals to re-initiate play after one or both of the play partners have paused, as strategic moves that allow a dog to position himself ready to either pounce upon or dodge his play partner, or, because play bows are often offered simultaneously, as a way to synchronize play behavior.

Play Synchronization?

The Study: Because it is quite possible that play bows are highly flexible signals and may have multiple functions, the researchers searched for evidence for all of the aforementioned possibilities. They presented four hypotheses regarding the function of the play bow: (1) To clarify play intentions; (2) To reinitiate play after a pause; (3) To position oneself for escape or attack; (4) To synchronize play behaviors. They also studied the role of the play bow as a distinctly visual signal, which if true, would mean that play bows are only offered when a dog is within the visual field of his or her play partner.

The team analyzed a set of videotaped play sessions of 16 dogs playing as pairs. The dogs were playing in either large enclosed backyards or a public area. All of the dogs were well socialized, played well together, and varied in their degree of familiarity with one another. Some had just recently met while others were well-acquainted friends. Play behaviors were coded according to a previously developed ethogram of adult dog behavior and were independently recorded by three reviewers. The number of play bows, their context, and each dog's behavior before, during and after play bows were recorded.

Results: A total of 414 play bows occurred during 22 separate play sessions. Four play pairs were responsible for the majority of the play bows (76 %). By comparison, no other pair accounted for more than 5 percent of total bows, suggesting that play bows vary dramatically among individuals and play pairs. There was no indication of an influence of age, sex or size influencing the number or form of play bows. However, this may be due to the relatively small sample size and are factors that could be examined in future work.

The collected data suggested the following regarding the function of play bowing for adult dogs during play:

* Both bowing dogs and their partners showed an increase in active play behavior following a play bow, supporting the hypothesis that *play bows function to reinitiate play following a pause.*

* The type of behaviors that dogs showed prior to and immediately following play bows tended to be similar within pairs, suggesting that play bows also help play partners to synchronize behavior. These results are corroborated by another recent study showing that dogs who use play bow mimicry tend to play together longer than those who do not (3).

* More than 98 percent, virtually all, of the play bows occurred when the two dogs were within each other's visual fields, providing strong support for the hypothesis that play bowing is an intentional visual signal that dogs only use when they know that their partner can see them and respond.

* Although the researchers did not find support for Bekoff's theory of the play bow as an intention clarifying signal, they note that his work was primarily with puppies and young dogs, and used a different methodology. It is possible that the bow serves this function for young dogs while they are ini-

150

tially learning to play and to inhibit their bite, and that this function is less necessary for adult dogs.

- Of the 16 dogs in this study, a single individual, a Belgian Tervuren named Tex, played with five different dogs and was responsible for more than 40 percent of the total play bows counted in the study. In contrast, several dogs showed just one play bow in a session or did not bow at all.

Take Away for Dog Folks: For dog folks, play bows are a welcome sight during paired or group play among adult dogs because we seem to intuitively grasp their use as a non-threatening and friendly signal. This new research, coupled with the earlier work of Marc Bekoff, suggests that bowing during play is not a random event that is just part of play, but rather that it is used to communicate specific information. For adults, this seems to be an invitation to continue play - *"Hey pal, let's start playing again!"* - as well as perhaps a way to coordinate and synchronize movement *"Okay Charlie, let's bow together and when I say GO, you shall zig and I shall zag"*. And for young dogs and perhaps some adults, it may also serve to clarify playful intent.

An additional important piece of information from this work is that play bows may be highly individual. Just a few pairs in the study used multiple bows and a single dog, Tex, apparently was bowing all over the place. I bet many of you are nodding right now. Because anecdotally, many of us have seen this in our own dogs or in dogs we work with. In the play group at my school, Colbie, a young Pit Bull, is a champion play-bower. She offers not only multiple play bows during paired and group play sessions, but she offers them at record speed, seemingly as an invitation to chase. My five-year-old Golden, Cooper, also bows during play, but (again anecdotal), he seems to bow most frequently when he plays with dogs who he knows well such as his housemates, and is less likely to play bow during group play.

Like all good research, this new study stimulates thought and additional questions to ask about the play bow. For example, what factors might influence a dog's frequent use of the bow - is it age, personality traits such as level of confidence or degree of playfulness, degree of familiarity among the dogs? Are there possibly learned components, such as training the play bow on cue? Does the use of a play bow ever "end badly"? In other words, do some dogs misinterpret this ubiquitous signal?

Lots to learn, and I am looking forward to seeing more from this team of researchers. Until then, play on, dogs, play on.

Cited Studies:

1. Byosiere SE, Espinosa J, Smuts B. Investigating the function of play bows in adult pet dogs (*Canis lupus familiaris*). *Behavioural Processes* 2016; 125:106-113.

2. Bekoff M. Play signals as punctuation: The structure of social play in canids. *Behaviour* 1995; 132:5-6.

3. Palagi E, Nicotra V, Cordoni G. Rapid mimicry and emotional contagion in domestic dogs. *Royal Society of Open Science* 2:150505; http://dx.doi.org/10.1098/rsos /150505.

24
I Feel Your Pain

Do dogs show empathy for their doggy friends? New research explores our dogs' altruistic nature.

Many people who live with multiple dogs have had the pleasure of experiencing two dogs who become great friends. Call the relationship what you will - bonded pair, social partners, housemates, doggy pals - I personally prefer friends, but hey, tomato/tomato, agreed? Regardless of what you label it, it is without question that dogs are highly social, that they bond with others in their social group, and that some dogs bond very strongly to each other.

The Emotional Lives of Dogs: It is (finally) accepted by scientists that dogs, like many other species, express a wide range of basic emotions. These include, but may not be limited to, fear, anxiety, jealousy, pleasure, playfulness, and happiness. (I would also add joy and silliness to these, but then, I live with a Toller).

What about Empathy? Seeing that dogs are highly social and that they bond closely to their companions, it is not a big jump to ask whether or not they are capable of feeling concern for others. At its most basic, empathy refers to the ability to share the emotions of another individual. However, there is debate over whether or not the expression of empathy must involve the capacity to take the perspective of the other, a level of cognition that requires at least a rudimentary "*theory of mind*". One approach to resolving this debate has been to classify empathy into several types, each requiring different levels of cognitive complexity.

- *Emotional contagion*, at the lowest level, refers to simply being affected by and sharing another's emotional state. This form of empathy has been found to exist in a wide variety of species, ***including dogs***.

- The next step up, *sympathetic concern* is expressed through comforting behaviors. The subject not only feels the other's emotions, but attempts to provide comfort to alleviate the other individual's distress. This level of empathy as well has been demonstrated in a wide range of species. Chimpanzees, some species of birds, ***and dogs*** all have been shown to demonstrate comforting behaviors towards others in distress.

- At the peak of the cognitive scale is *empathic perspective,* which requires the capacity to understand and appraise a situation from the other individual's point of view. An example of this is prosocial helping, a talent ***that dogs*** have indeed been found to be capable of when they are made aware of their owner's goal. (This research is reviewed in my previous book, *"Beware the Straw Man"*).

Once Again, It is All about Us: So, one might be inclined to stop here, seeing that there is certainly scientific evidence of empathic responses in dogs. But herein lies the rub. All of this previous work examined not if dogs respond empathically to other dogs, but rather, how dogs recognize and respond to the emotional state of *humans*. This is all very cool work, for sure, but it is a rather odd state of affairs since all of the research with other species such as Chimpanzees, Bonobos, birds, and even elephants have examined empathic responses among con-specifics - members of the same species. Most of the results in those animals have also reported that individuals are much more likely to demonstrate empathy (at any level) for a close relative or a member of their social group than for an unfamiliar individual.

Do Dogs Care about Their Friends? Do we know anything about how dogs react to the distress of other dogs? If they do show empathy, will they react more dramatically to a dog friend versus an unfamiliar dog? Recently, a group of researchers at the University of Vienna in Austria and at the Comparative Ethology Research Group in Budapest Hungary collaborated and asked exactly these questions (1).

The Study: Sixteen pairs of dogs who had lived together in the same home for at least one year were studied. Within each pair, one dog was randomly assigned to be the subject and the other to be the "distressed" partner. The partner's stress whine was pre-recorded and used during the experiment. Each subject dog was studied under three conditions, spaced apart by 2-week intervals: (1) the whine of their (absent) household partner; (2) the whine of an unfamiliar dog; and (3) a recording of computer-generated sounds with a cadence and frequency similar to dog whines (the control). The subject dog's physiological response (heart rate and salivary cortisol levels) and behavioral response (stress signals) were recorded before and after listening to the recorded sounds, which came from behind an opaque screen. At the end of each period, the partner dog was immediately brought into the room, apparently from behind the screen (the reunion phase) and the subject dog's behavior upon seeing his or her housemate was also recorded. (You can imagine how this would feel....."*Dude! What were they doing to you back there??!!!*")

Results: The dogs in this study definitely reacted to the distress calls of another dog. Upon hearing whining from behind the screen, the dogs spent significantly more time gazing towards the source of the cries and moving closer to the screen than they did when exposed to the non-dog control sounds. This should certainly not be surprising to most dog folks. In addition, this study also provided a few other interesting results:

- **Dogs care about other dogs:** The dogs expressed more anxiety and stress behaviors when they listened to the recorded cries of their housemate or an unfamiliar dog compared to when they were listening to the control sounds.

- **Expressing their concern:** When dogs were reunited with their partners, they spent more time with their friend and showed more affiliative (loving) behaviors towards their partner dog after having heard a recording of the partner's whine compared to when they had heard an unfamiliar whine or the control sounds.

- **Feeling stressed:** Hearing their friend whining also caused dogs' salivary cortisol levels to remain elevated during the testing conditions, suggesting that they were more highly stressed upon hearing the distress of their friend compared to their stress level during the control condition.

Take Away for Dog Folks: This study, the first to directly measure dogs' empathic response to other dogs, provides evidence that dogs are capable of the first level of empathy, emotional contagion. The dogs were clearly affected by and shared the distressed emotional state of a dog who they could hear but not see. The study also showed us that dogs recognize and respond to the distress of a friend more intensely than they do to that of a dog who they do not know and that they show strong affiliative behaviors towards their friend upon being reunited. These behaviors suggest that not only do dogs recognize the vocalizations of their friends (which has been demonstrated in other studies) but that they express the second level of empathy - sympathetic concern.

Anecdotes about dogs who love each other and who express distress and concern for their friends abound. Personally, I too carry the belief that dogs, as highly social beings, care for and are concerned about the welfare of their canine buddies. Now we have a bit of research to support this, continuing to expand our understanding of our dogs and about what matters to them in their lives.

Cited Study: Quervel-Chaumette M, Faerber V, Farago T, Marshall-Pescini S, Range F. Investigating empathy-like responding to conspecifics' distress in pet dogs. *PLOS-One* 2016; 11 (4):e0152920. DOI: 10.1371/journal.pone.0152920.

25
Our Best Friends' Friends

A bit of evidence against the age-old myths about dogs and cats.

Our five-year-old Golden, Cooper has a friend named Pete. Cooper and Pete groom each other, take naps together on a favorite bed, and play their own special version of "wolf and caribou" around the dining room table. When Coop goes on walks, he likes to have Pete come along with us.

And oh yeah, Pete is our cat.

Many folks who live with dogs and cats are not surprised by this friendship and have great stories of their own to tell about a special bond between a dog and cat. However, the myth that dogs do not particularly like cats certainly continues to persist. Likewise, it is generally accepted that not all cats are pleased about having to share their home with a dog.

The underlying foundation for the assumption that dogs and cats cannot be friends is perhaps the fact that they are vastly dissimilar species, with different evolutionary histories, social behaviors and communication patterns. Regardless, anecdotal evidence abounds about the ability of individuals from the two species to form close and enduring friendships. And, I found recently, there is even a bit of science to back up these stories.

The Study: A group of investigators from Tel Aviv University in Israel interviewed 170 pet owners who lived with both a dog and a cat (1). The study also included direct observations of the pets in 45 of the homes.

Results: Not only do dogs and cats get along well, they also appear to be able to learn quite a bit about communicating with each other:

- The majority of the owners (> 60 %) reported that their dog and cat were amicable and friendly toward each other and less than 1 in 10 owners reported aggressive behaviors. (The remaining pets were largely indifferent to each other).

- Mutual play made up a substantial proportion of the interactions between dogs and cats, as did staying in the same room or resting and sleeping together. Interestingly, the cats in the study offered significantly more play soliciting behaviors to their dog friends than vice versa.

- Perhaps not surprisingly, the two factors that were found to be important determinants for influencing the dog/cat relationship were the order of adoption (friendships were more likely when cats were adopted first) and age of adoption (friendships were more likely when both animals were adopted when they were young).

Take Away for Dog (and Cat) Folks: One of the most interesting results from this study had to do with the types of communication signals that were used by the dog and cat friends. More than 75 % of the greeting behaviors between these friends occurred in the form of a "nose-touch", which is considered to be a common feline-specific greeting pattern, rather than a canine-specific greeting signal.

The researchers also reported several communication signals that had an unrelated or opposite meaning to the other species, yet were still correctly interpreted by the receiving animal. Examples of these included lying on the back (submission or play in dogs versus aggression or predation in cats) and stretching out the forefeet (play in dogs versus aggression in cats). This is pretty cool stuff as it suggests that dogs and cats who share a home and become friends not only enjoy hanging out, playing, and resting together, but also appear to learn each other's body language, even when certain signals may mean something very different in their own species.

As for Pete and Cooper, they say, "*Yeah? No big surprise at all!*"

Cited Study: Feuersten N, Terkel J. Interrelationships of dogs (*Canis familiaris*) and cats (*Felis catus*) living under the same roof. *Applied Animal Behaviour Science* 2008; 113:150-165.

Part 3 –
Stirring Things Up

26
Death Throes of the Guilty Look

A series of cleverly designed studies should put the "my dog is guilty" claim to rest, once and for all.

I recently talked to a potential client who is interested in bringing his 7-month-old Golden Doodle to train with us at Autumn-Gold. His dog, Penny, has the usual young dog issues - jumping up, a bit of nipping during play, still the occasional slip in house training, etc. Penny also raids the kitchen garbage bin, removing and shredding food wrappers, napkins, and any other paper goodies that she can find. The owner told me that he is particularly upset about this last behavior because he is certain that Penny *"knows she has done wrong"*. He knows this because..... wait for it ...."*Penny always looks guilty when he confronts her about what she did"*.

If I had a nickel.........

Like many trainers, I repeatedly and often futilely it seems, explain to owners that what they are more likely witnessing in these circumstances is their dog communicating signs of appeasement, submission, or even fear. And, also like many other trainers, I often feel as though I am beating my head against the proverbial wall.

But wait! Once again, science comes to our rescue! And this time, it is a darned good rescue indeed because there is quite a bit of recent of evidence about this issue.

The Studies: The guilty look is a difficult issue to study because it requires that researchers identify and test all of the potential triggers that may elicit it, as well as the influence the owner's behavior and his or her perceptions of their dog may have.

162

Tricky stuff, but lucky for us, several teams of researchers have tackled this in recent years, using a series of cleverly designed experiments.

Study 1: Is it scolding owners? The first study, published in 2009, was designed to determine if dogs who show the "guilty look" (hereafter, the GL) are demonstrating contrition because they misbehaved or rather are reacting to their owner's cues, having learned from previous experience that certain owner behaviors signal anger and predict impending punishment (1).

The study used a 2x2 factorial design, in which dogs were manipulated to either obey or disobey their owner's command to not eat a desirable treat and owners, who were not present at the time, were informed either correctly or incorrectly of their dog's behavior. The diagram below illustrates the four possible scenario combinations:

Four Treatment Groups in Study 1

Study design: Fourteen dogs were enrolled and testing took place in the owner's home. All of the owners had used "scolding" to punish their dogs in the past and an additional one in five also admitted that they used physical reprimands such as forced downs, spanking, or grabbing their dog's scruff. All of the dogs were pre-tested to ensure that they had been trained to respond reliably to a "leave it" command and would refrain from eating a treat on their owner's instruction. During each test scenario, the owner placed a treat on the ground, commanded the dog to "leave it", and then left the room. While the owner was out of the room, the experimenter picked up the treat and either (1) gave the treat to the dog or (2) removed the treat. Upon returning to the room the owner was informed (correctly or incorrectly) about their dog's behavior while they were away. Each dog was tested in all four possible combinations. Test sessions were videotaped and dogs' responses were analyzed for the presence and absence of behaviors that are associated with the GL in each of the four situations.

The Results: Two important results came from this study:

1. Scolding by the owner was highly likely to cause a dog to exhibit a GL, *regardless of whether or not the dog had eaten the treat in the owner's absence.*

2. Dogs were not more likely to show a GL after having disobeyed their owner than when they had obeyed. In other words, having disobeyed their owner's command was not the primary factor that predicted whether or not a dog showed a GL.

First nail in the coffin –
The owner's behavior can trigger the GL.

What about dogs who "tell" on themselves? But wait, Joe next door (who happens to know a lot about dogs) says - *"How do you explain my dog Muffin who greets me at the door, groveling and showing a GL, before I even know that she has done something wrong?"*

Not to worry - The scientists got this one too.

Study 2: Experimenters set up a series of scenarios involving 64 dog/owner pairs (2). The testing took place individually in a neutral room with just the dog, the owner and the researcher present. After acclimatizing to the room and meeting the experimenter, the dog was commanded by the owners to "leave" a piece of hot dog that was left sitting on a table. The owner then left the room. In this experimental design, the experimenters did not manipulate the dog's response. Instead, they simply recorded whether the dog took the treat or not. Before calling the owner back into the room, the treat (if not eaten) was removed. The owner then returned to the room but was not informed about what the dog did (or did not) do in their absence. The owner then was asked to determine, by their *dog's behavior* whether or not the dog had obeyed their command. In this way, the experimenters ingeniously tested for the "*dog telling on himself*" possibility.

Results: Just as the first study found, a dog's behavior in the owner's absence was not correlated with showing a GL upon the owner's return. (Corroborating evidence from independent studies is always a good thing). The researchers also found that when they controlled for expectations, owners were unable to accurately determine whether or not their dog had disobeyed while they were out of the room, based only upon the dog's greeting behavior. In other words, the claim that dogs tell on themselves and therefore must have an understanding that they had misbehaved was not supported.

Second nail in the coffin –
Dogs don't really tell on themselves (it's an owner's myth)

The next study, published in 2015, parsed out the final two factors that could be involved in the infamous GL - the presence of evidence as a trigger and guilt itself.

Study 3: If indeed, as many owners insist, a dog's demonstration of the GL is based upon the dog having an understanding of the "wrongness" of an earlier action, then this would mean that the trigger for the GL would have to be directly linked to the dog's actual *commitment of the wrongful act,* correct? Likewise, if the dog herself did *not* commit a misdeed, then she should not be feeling guilty and so should not demonstrate a GL to the owner. It is also possible that the mere presence of evidence from a misdeed (for example, a dumped over garbage tin) could become a learned cue that predicts eventual punishment to the dog. In this case, a dog would be expected to show a GL in the presence

166

of the evidence, regardless of whether or not he or she was personally responsible for it.

This study tested both of these factors (3). Using a similar procedure to those previously described, the researchers created scenarios in which dogs either did or did not eat a forbidden treat in their owner's absence. They then either kept the evidence present or removed it prior to the owner's return to the room. Owners were instructed to greet their dog in a friendly manner and to determine whether or not their dog had misbehaved based only upon their dog's behavior.

Results: Owners were unable to accurately determine whether or not their dog had misbehaved based upon their dog's greeting behavior. Moreover, the dogs' actions did not increase or decrease their inclination to greet the owner showing a GL. A dog's inclination to demonstrate a GL was also not influenced one way or the other by the presence of evidence. This second finding suggests that the presence of evidence is not an important (learned) trigger for the GL in dogs. Rather the strongest factor that influences whether or not a dog exhibits a GL upon greeting appears to be the owner's behavior.

Third and final nail –
Neither engaging in a misdeed nor seeing evidence of a misdeed accurately predict whether or not a dog will show a GL.

Ding Dong, The Guilty Look is Dead!

Take Away for Dog Folks: This series of studies tells us that at least some dogs who show signs of appeasement, submission or fear (aka the GL) upon greeting their owners will do so regardless of whether or not they misbehaved in their owner's absence. We also know that an owner's behavior and use of scolding and reprimands are the *most* significant predictor of this type of greeting behavior in dogs. These results should really be the final death throes of belief in the GL.

Good Riddance to it, I say.

Now, all that needs to be done is that trainers, behaviorists and dog professionals everywhere work to educate and encourage all dog owners to Please, please **Stop Doing This:**

Cited Studies:

1. Horowitz A. Disambiguating the "guilty look": Salient prompts to a familiar dog behavior. *Behavioural Processes* 2009; 81:447-452.

2. Hecht J, Miklosi A, Gacsi M. Behavioral assessment and owner perceptions of behaviors associated with guilty in dogs. *Applied Animal Behavior Science* 2012; 139:134-142.

3. Ostojic L, Tkalcic M, Clayton N. Are owners' reports of their dogs' "guilty look" influenced by the dogs' action and evidence of the misdeed? *Behavioural Processes* 2015; 111:97-100.

27
How Many Barks Does a Nuisance Dog Make?

How we label a dog's behavior influences how we think about it and how we decide to treat it.

According to a paper that I read recently, *nuisance barking* is identified as a major, worldwide behavior problem that affects one in three dogs, is a frequent cause of neighbor disputes, and is a common cause of relinquishment of dogs by their owners to shelters and rescue groups (1).

Hmmm.... *Nuisance barking.*

So, once again, it is all about us. Because really, if we asked the dogs to tell us why they are barking, I would venture that the vast majority would NOT say: "***Oh, because I want to be a nuisance***".

Rather (and I know you trainers and behaviorists are with me on this one), their reasons, in no particular order, are much more likely to be:

1. I am bored because I spend too much time alone.
2. I am stressed because I am uncomfortable being alone.
3. I feel territorial around my home's doors, windows, or yard.
4. I am responding to noises in my neighborhood such as other dogs barking, vehicles approaching or people walking by.
5. I am responding to the sight of people or other animals outside or near my home.

So, let me begin by saying, up front, that I was irritated by the title of this paper and the authors' casual acceptance of the term *nuisance barking*. And yes, I know that the term can function as a way of classifying what people tell others and also how some animal control agencies handle barking complaints. However, if the place at which we begin is by classifying any barking that an owner (or neighbor) does not like in terms of human comfort and perspective, where exactly does that lead us regarding how we think about *the dogs* who are doing this barking? (Remember the Ben Franklin effect from *"Beware the Straw Man"*?) I would argue that the term *nuisance barking* itself is highly pejorative because once such a label is applied you now have a *bad dog* who needs correcting or a bark collar or relinquishment to a shelter. Because heavens, we certainly cannot live with a nuisance in our lives, can we now?

The good news is that once that rant was out of my system, I went on to read an interesting study. Here is what they did:

The Study: Study participants were 25 dogs who had been identified by their owners as being guilty of the nefarious deed "*nuisance barking*." The researchers were interested in determining the actual frequencies and durations of this type of barking and if there were clear factors in a dog's life or behavior that were related. They studied this using a bark counter, a device that when mounted on a dog's collar will record the duration, frequency and number of distinct barks throughout a pre-designated period. Each dog was fitted with a counter and barking was recorded continuously over a 7-day period. All of the owners also completed a questionnaire that provided information about themselves and their dog.

Results: A wide range of bark frequencies and durations were recorded. For example, frequencies ranged from 10 to more than 500 barks in an hour. Dogs barked most often when their owner was away and the majority of the dogs in the sample (84 %) were confined to a yard or garden area when the owner was not at home. (Hmmm.....might these two things be related?).

Bark patterns throughout the day suggested that much of the barking was reactive - dogs were responding to one or more stimuli in their environment. When asked, many of the owners could readily identify the cause. The most frequently cited stimuli were the presence of people or other animals as they passed by the dog's yard. (In other words, many owners already knew exactly what was causing their dog to bark).

Although few significant factors in dogs' lives were found to influence barking (possibly because of the small sample size), the researchers did find a negative association between the amount of obedience training that a dog had received and degree of barking; dogs who had received training had lower barking frequencies than dogs who had not. A weak association was also found between the number of neighboring dogs and barking; dogs who lived near several other dogs were more likely to bark than dogs who did not. (And there's a second environmental stimulus.....).

Take Away for Dog Folks: First, let's forget the "*nuisance*" label. It is a red herring. Please stop using that word.

Second, it is significant that the owners of the dogs enrolled in this study were able to identify at least one clear underlying cause of their dog's excessive barking (the presence of passersby near the dog's yard). Neighboring dogs were apparently also a trigger for some dogs.

It seems to me we have more of an owner problem here than a dog problem. These data suggest that reactive barking is a common cause of excessive barking in dogs who are isolated in yards. And, lo and behold, there are several tried and true methods for reducing territorial or reactive barking in dogs (it really ain't rocket science). These include:

1. Reduce the time that the dog spends isolated in the yard.

2. Train an alternative behavior (response substitution), such as coming away from the barrier (fence, property edge).

172

3. Manage the behavior by preventing the dog's ability to see/hear the triggering stimuli (privacy screens, *bring the dog indoors*).

4. Increase the dog's daily exercise, mental and emotional stimulation so that the dog spends less time isolated in the yard (if necessary hire a dog walker or use a reputable doggy day care).

Up on my Soapbox

I am back in my snit, it appears. It is my contention that dogs and their people are much better served if we stop using anthropocentric classifications for problem behaviors that label dogs as nuisances. Rather, as this study corroborates, dogs bark for reasons and often these reasons are something that we can remove, modify or manage. If we begin the discussion with "*I have a nuisance dog who barks too much*" we have all the further to go towards changing perspective and identifying the cause so that we can start helping both the dog and the owner.

Because dogs bark. And some dogs bark a lot. Maybe too much. Just like people talk and some people certainly talk too much.... (You know these people, the *nuisance talkers*. For those people in your life, you are on your own). For the dogs, I am with all of the trainers out there who start by finding out *why* the dog is barking, eliminating or modifying that cause, adding in a bit of training, exercising, and playing, with the ultimate goal of a happy dog whose owner never considers labeling him as a *nuisance.*

Cited Study: Raglus TI, Groef BD, Marston LC. Can bark counter collars and owner surveys help identify factors that relate to nuisance barking? A pilot study. *Journal of Veterinary Behavior* 2015; 10:204-209.

28
A Walk in the Park (or not)

What are the exercise and emotional benefits of walking dogs? Are those exercise benefits observed in dog parks?

In my view, one of the many benefits of living with dogs are the walks. All four of my dogs love to hike and run and we spend time together almost every morning at our local forest preserve. The dogs enjoy the exercise and have opportunities to explore, sniff and play, while Mike and I exercise, enjoy the outdoors and spend quality time with our family.

Dog walks can also be social events. A friend and I meet regularly at different parks to hike with our dogs. We enjoy exploring new trails and rotate favorite parks so that the dogs experience and enjoy a variety of outdoor areas. Group walks are also a regular part of AutumnGold's open floor training nights and are great fun for dogs and their people.

AutumnGold Trainers Enjoy a Group Dog Walk

For dog folks, it comes as no surprise that this activity is good for us. There is ample evidence that, as a group, dog owners are more physically active than are non-owners and that acquiring a dog often leads to an increase in activity level. Other studies have found that dog owners report physical *and* psychosocial benefits of walking with their dogs. They get to know other dog walkers in their area, have increased opportunities to meet new people, and develop a sense of community in their neighborhoods. All proven stuff, and not all that noteworthy, since the social and emotional benefits of dog ownership have been known for many years.

The Paradox: However, herein lies the paradox. Although American dog owners are more likely to engage in regular walking than are non-owners, the actual proportion of owners who walk their dogs is quite low. While more than 45 percent of homes in the US have one or more dogs, *less than 3 percent* of Americans walk their dog for 30 minutes or more per day and between 40 and 60 percent of dog owners do not walk their dogs at all (1).

Why Should You Care? Well, because walking briskly for 30 minutes daily can achieve the current recommendations for regular physical activity for adults - a level that is seriously underachieved by many Americans. Knowing this, several public health researchers have recently identified dog walking as a viable approach to improving the physical activity of adults in populations that are notably under-exercising.

And, being researchers, they then proceeded to do what researchers do.......They studied dog walking.

How Much Dog Walking Does it Take? Elizabeth Richards and a team of researchers at Purdue University were the first to directly measure the frequency and the intensity of dog walking using activity monitors (think Fit Bit) (2). They outfitted a group of 65 dog owners with accelerometers and collected data over a 7-day period. Owners wore the monitors continuously and recorded the time of day that they started and ended their dog walks.

Results: Participants walked their dogs at least one time per day and averaged approximately 30 minutes per walk. During dog walks, almost 80 percent of the exercise was classified as "moderate-vigorous physical activity" (MVPA). About 14 percent of the time was classified as light intensity and 4 percent was sedentary (that must have been the poop stops). The majority of the periods of MVPA occurred in bouts of time that were more than 10 minutes. These distinctions are important because current physical activity guidelines for Americans specify 150 minutes of MVPA per week, achieved in bouts of 10 minutes or more at a time. The authors conclude that: "....*dog walking is a type of physical activity that merits greater attention from public health officials and practitioners. Increasing the prevalence of dog walking could help the US attain physical activity objectives....*"

Who's Walking (and Why)? The Purdue study (among others) provides evidence that dog walking can be a great form of exercise (for dogs and humans). Carri Westgarth and colleagues at the University of Liverpool tackled the next question: *What are some of the personal and societal factors that influence an owner's inclination to walk regularly (or not) with his or her dog?* They conducted a systematic review of 31 studies that examined dog ownership and dog walking, published over a 22-year period (3).

Results: They found that the dedicated dog walkers tend to be owners who possess a strong sense of obligation to their dog's need for regular exercise and who report that their dog is an important motivator, both for the owner to be active and for spending quality time with their dog. Community factors that are most important include accessibility to public areas that are suitable for walking, that allow off-leash exercise for dogs, and that are designed to promote social interactions with other people.

Most interesting perhaps is the authors' conclusion regarding dog walking areas: "*The design of areas intended for dog walking and how they fulfill dog and owner needs may be an important consideration for future interventions. In order to encourage more dog owners to walk their dogs, the recreational areas used for dog walking must be both pleasurable and accessible, as opposed to the common phenomenon of relegating dog access only to the few areas left after other user types have been accommodated.*"

From this conclusion, it follows that one may ponder.........

What about Dog Parks? It is logical to ask if the increased number and popularity of dog parks in recent years has contributed to dog walking frequency among dog owners. To date only a few studies have examined this relationship. Most recently, Kelly Evenson and several colleagues studied the activity level of dog owners at six different dog parks located in North Carolina, California and Pennsylvania (4). They used a validated measurement tool (The Systematic Observation of Play and Recreation in Communities) to count visitors and monitor activity levels over a one-week period. The researchers also directly interviewed 604 dog park visitors.

Results: The primary activity of people who were visiting the dog parks was standing without moving. A whopping *79 percent* of the recorded activity of dog park visitors was classified as sedentary. Only 20 percent was the activity was walking, and almost none (1 percent) was classified as vigorous. To make matters worse, the majority of owners (70.4 %) drove their dog to the park, even though many lived less than a mile away. These results were in agreement with two previous studies that collectively examined more than 30 dog parks in multiple states. The authors conclude: "*This study......revealed that dog park visitors more often engaged in sedentary behavior or standing without moving than did visitors to other areas of the park......*"

Take Away for Dog Folks: For trainers, veterinarians, behaviorists and other dog professionals, the take away from this research is that we should encourage our clients to walk with their dogs, not only for the many benefits that the dogs will enjoy, but to take advantage of the health benefits for themselves. This seems like a no-brainer and is a win-win for dogs and people both. Additionally, we can advocate for more accessible, dog-friendly walking areas in our communities.

By this, I do *not* mean more dog parks.

Up on my Soapbox

Out Comes the Ol' Box: In case you think this is going to be a rant from an exercise fanatic who thinks every dog park visitor should get off of her duff and start lapping the park periphery with their Border Collie, well, that is not where this is going at all. (Though, I was tempted).

Rather, here is my issue regarding the evidence from these studies. The Westgarth study makes the point that one way to encourage dog owners to walk more with their dogs (or to walk at all with their dogs) is to provide areas in communities that are specifically designed for dog walking. They address the need for areas that are pleasurable places to walk (i.e. have trails and paths), are accessible, and of course are welcoming to dogs. In other words.......*parks*. Most *dog* parks provide none of this stuff. As described in the Evenson study, many dog parks are small areas, usually less than a few acres, and are relegated to crappy bits of land that were either not suitable for any other type of use or are adjacent to larger and more attractive public parks.

Evenson's paper provides evidence of this. All of the six sites that they studied were small (less than 2 acres) and were adjacent to parks that were used for other human recreation purposes. Of the six dog parks, the authors noted that three were developed on land that was located beneath or near power lines, and all six were located adjacent to, across the street from, or almost a mile away from the public park. Given their small sizes, none of these dog parks could provide walking opportunities for people and their dogs.

I know that some people will respond that they do not go to the dog park for their own exercise, but rather they go so that their dog can play and romp off-lead and can interact (for good or for bad) with other dogs. I completely understand the benefits of allowing dogs to have off-lead play time and personally love to hike with my own dogs off-lead. I also know that dog parks can be dangerous places to allow dogs off-lead play time. (If you doubt this, see the evidence provided in my previous book, *Beware the Straw Man"*). However, regardless of my opinion regarding the safety of dog parks, my point in *this* essay is that the over-emphasis of dog parks in communities, parks that are often small and undesirable snippets of land, can lead to the further segregation of our dogs from the rest of society and certainly will not encourage dog walks and the positive benefits that they have for dogs and owners alike.

So, if you love your dog park and are now in a snit regarding this evidence (and my opinion), let me ask this: If you frequent dog parks with your dog, do you *also* take him walking with you, on new routes around your neighborhood, or to area walking paths and parks, so that you can walk *together* and enjoy exercising with your dog? If not, you should. Because the evidence shows that dog parks ain't doin' it for us.

Cited Studies:

1. Richards EA, McDonough M, Edwards N, Lyle R, roped PJ. Psychosocial and environmental factors associated with dog walking. *International Journal of Health Promotion and Education* 2013; 51:198-211.

2. Richards EA, Troped PJ, Lim E. Assessing the intensity of dog walking and impact on overall physical activity: A pilot study using accelerometry. *Open Journal of Preventive Medicine* 2014; 4:523-528.

3. Westgarth C, Christley RM, Christian HE. How might we increase physical activity through dog walking? A comprehensive review of dog walking correlates. *International Journal of Behavioral Nutrition and Physical Activity* 2014; 11:83-97.

4. Evenson KR, Shay E, Williamson S, Cohen DA. Use of dog parks and the contribution to physical activity for their owners. *Research Quarterly for Exercise and Sport* 2016; March 1; 1-9.

29
Pretty in Pink

Breed stereotypes reduce a dog's chance of adoption and increase risk of euthanasia, concerning facts when there is a lack of consensus about breed identification.

Our youngest dog, Ally, has a 'bestie". Her name is Colbie and she belongs to our friend Amanda, a trainer who works as an instructor at AutumnGold. Ally is a Golden Retriever. Colbie is a Pit Bull Terrier, adopted from our local shelter while Amanda was on staff there.

Being young girls, both Ally and Colbie wear pink collars, Gentle Leaders and harnesses. For Ally, this is simply a fashion statement. For Colbie, given her breed and the breed-stereotypes that she may encounter, it means a bit more. Amanda purposefully dresses Colbie in pink hoping that such feminine attire will present Colbie as the sweetheart that she is. (Being color-blind, Colbie has no opinion).

Although Ally does not care about Colbie's genetic heritage (or that she wears pink), many people do. Breed stereotypes are pervasive and impact local and state breed-specific legislation (BSL), rental property regulations, and shelter decisions regarding adoption and euthanasia. BSLs in the US and UK specifically target Pit Bull Terriers and other bully-type breeds, and either ban ownership of these breeds outright or impose strict restrictions upon ownership. These laws are based upon the assumption that targeted breeds are inherently dangerous and that individuals of the breeds can be reliably identified. There is much controversy (and no consensus) regarding the first assumption and is a topic for another time. In this essay, we look at the second assumption regarding reliable breed identification. Is there supporting evidence? It turns out that there is quite a bit of science on this topic - and the results are quite revealing.

Pit Bull or Something Else? Prior to the development of reliable DNA testing, the only method available for identifying the breed of a dog whose heritage was unknown was visual assessment. A shelter worker, veterinarian or animal control officer examines the dog and assigns a breed designation based upon physical appearance and conformation. Even with widespread availability of reliable DNA tests, most shelters and rescue groups continue to rely upon visual identification to assign breed labels to the dogs in their care. Given the life or death import of these decisions for some dogs, it is odd that the question of the reliability of these evaluations has not been questioned.

Until recently.

Experts Don't Agree: In 2013, Victoria Voith and her co-researchers asked over 900 pet professionals to assign a breed (or mix of breeds) to 20 dogs that they viewed on one-minute video clips (1). Each of the dogs underwent DNA testing prior to the study, which allowed the researchers to test both the accuracy of visual breed-identification and the degree of agreement among the dog experts.

Results: Poor agreement was found between visual breed assignments and DNA results in 14 of the 20 dogs (**70 %**). Moreover, there was low inter-rater reliability, meaning that the dog experts did not show a high level of agreement regarding breed assignments to the 20 dogs. More than half of the evaluators agreed on the predominant breed in only 7 of the 20 dogs (35%). Although Pit Bull Terriers were not specifically examined in this study, these results provide *evidence that physical appearance is not a reliable method for breed identification.*

You say Pit Bull, I say Boxer: The following year, researchers in the US and the UK collaborated and examined the consistency with which shelter works assigned breed labels to the dogs in their care (2). A group of 416 shelter works in the US and 54 in the UK were asked to assign a breed or mix of breeds to photographs of 20 dogs. They also completed a questionnaire that asked them to list the specific features that they used in their determination. Of the 20 dogs that were used in this study, more than 3/4 had a bully-breed appearance. (Note: An important difference between the UK and the US is that all UK shelters are subject to the country's Dangerous Dog Act, a law that bans the ownership of Pit Bulls. While such bans exist in the US, there is no universal law. Rather, select municipalities or states have various forms of BSL).

Results: Perhaps not surprisingly, UK shelter workers were much less likely to identify a dog with a "bully appearance" as a Pit Bull Terrier than were US shelter workers. Instead, the UK shelter workers tended to label these dogs as Staffordshire Bull Terriers, a breed that is allowed in the UK, rather than as a Pit Bull, a breed that is universally banned. Despite this difference, results corroborated Voith's study in that the *researchers found a great deal of variation among shelter workers in their assignments of breed and there was a lack of consensus regarding which of the 20 dogs were identifiable as Pit Bull Terriers.*

DNA vs. Shelter Staff: A 2015 study surveyed experienced shelter staff members at several Florida animal shelters (3). At each of four sites, four staff members were asked to assign breed designations to 30 adoptable dogs who were housed at their shelter. Collectively, 120 dogs were evaluated by 16 staff members. DNA testing was conducted on all of the dogs. A primary objective of this study was to examine the reliability of shelter staff's ability to identify Pit Bull Terriers and dogs with Pit Bull heritage and to compare their assessments with DNA results. (Note: The DNA signatures that are used to identify Pit Bull Terriers are those of the American Staffordshire Terrier and the Staffordshire Bull

Terriers, two breeds that are considered to be genetically identical to the Pit Bull Terrier).

Results: Approximately *one-third* of the dogs who were identified as a pit bull-type breed by one or more shelter staff lacked any DNA evidence of bully breeds in his/her heritage. When inter-rater reliability among the participants was examined, agreement among shelter staff was moderate, but still included a relatively large number of disagreements. What this means in practical terms is that a substantial number of dogs in this study were labeled as pit bulls or pit bull types and yet had no such genetic background. Even if the shelter staff agreed on a particular dog's identification, this would be rather a moot point (for the dog) if they both happened to be wrong.

But she doesn't *look* like a Chow Chow: How can this be? How is it possible that a dog who appears to have the characteristic "pittie-type" head shape, muscular body and other distinctive features tests negative for Pit Bull heritage? The conclusion that many people make from these discrepancies is that DNA testing must be unreliable, inaccurate, or just plain wrong. However, the fact is that it is not uncommon for the results of DNA tests of dogs who have a mixed heritage to identify a set of primary ancestor breeds that look nothing like the dog in question. This occurs because purebred crosses, particularly after the first generation, can result in unique combinations of genes that produce a wide range of features. When several different breeds are involved, some of these features may not be apparent in any of the ancestral breeds.

This occurs for two reasons. First, many of the breeds that we know today were originally created by crossing two or more existing breeds and then selecting for a small set of physically unique traits in subsequent generations. However, the dogs of these breeds still carry genes for a much wider variety of traits, even though the genes are not being "expressed" in the dog's appearance. When these dogs are then bred to dogs of other breeds the hidden traits may become evident in their puppies. A second reason is that less than 1 percent of the canine genome encodes for breed-specific traits such ear shape, coat type and color, and head shape. So, a dog could be a large part (genetically) of a certain breed, while not showing all of the breeds physical traits, which may have been rapidly lost during cross-breeding with other breeds.

What This Means for Dogs: These three studies provide valuable evidence that the use of visual assessments to assign breed or breed-mixes to dogs is inaccurate and unreliable. Not to put too fine a point on it, but this information is of more than just casual interest for dogs like Colbie. Pit Bull Terriers and the other "bully breeds" are most frequently stigmatized by breed stereotypes and impacted by BSL and shelter policies that require automatic euthanasia. It is not an exaggeration to suggest that identifying an individual dog as a Pit Bull may be a matter of life or death for that dog.

It is not an exaggeration because we now have evidence.

Researchers ask, "What' in a Name"? A recent paper published by researchers in Clive Wynne's dog lab at the University of Arizona describes an ambitious series of experiments in which they examined the impact of breed labels on the perceptions of potential adopters and on the eventual outcome for the dog. The studies were carried out online and at animal shelters in Florida and Arizona. Participants were asked to rate photographs, videotapes, or live dogs in their kennels. In some conditions the dogs were presented with a breed label and in others they were not.

Results: Two major findings came out of these studies. The first showed that stereotypes about Pit Bulls are alive and well and the second showed how this stigmatization ultimately affects dogs:

1. People rated an image of a "pit-bull-type" dog as less approachable, friendly and intelligent and as more aggressive when compared to an image of either a Labrador Retriever and a Border Collie. In another experiment, labeling a dog as a Pit Bull negatively influenced the perceptions that people had about the dog. When visitors rated a dog who was labeled as a Pit Bull, the dogs were found to be less attractive in terms of perceived approachability, friendliness, intelligence, aggressiveness and adoptability compared with when the *same dog* was not so labeled.

2. Dogs who had been labeled as Pit Bulls had length of stays in the Florida shelter prior to adoption that were over three times as long as the stays of dogs who were matched in appearance, but had been labeled as another breed or breed-mix. When breed labels were removed from the profile cards of dogs offered for adoption, adoption rates for Pit Bulls increased significantly, length of stays prior to adoption in the shelter decreased, as did euthanasia rates. Interestingly, not only pit-bull-type dogs benefited from removing breed labels from the kennel cards. Dogs from working breeds who were available for adoption, in particular Boxers, Dobermans and Mastiffs also showed an increase in adoption rate.

Take Away for Dog Folks: There is a lot to ponder here. We have learned that breed identification using a dog's physical appearance, even when conducted by experienced dog experts, is flawed in two distinctive ways. First, experts cannot agree consistently about how to label an individual dog. One person's Boxer-mix is another's Pit Bull and is yet another's Bulldog/Lab mix. Second, DNA tests do not consistently confirm breed assignments that were based upon physical appearance. Labeling breeds for purposes of shelter retention, adoption and euthanasia is a highly dubious process, and one that is most critical for Pit Bull Terriers and other bully breeds.

We have also learned that potential adopters react to a Pit Bull label in ways that may adversely affect the outcome for the dog. Labeling a dog as Pit Bull may increase her length of stay in the shelter, reduce her chances of adoption and increase her risk of being killed - simply because she was assigned a (possibly incorrect) label that changed the perceptions of potential adopters. And last, we have evidence that removing breed labels from the cage cards of adoptable pit-bull-type dogs (and many other dogs) increases their chance of adoption, reduces the length of their stay in the shelter, and increases their chance of simply staying alive.

Pretty in Pink for sure. But, I say, it is time that wearing pink becomes a simple fashion statement for Colbie, just as it is for her pal Ally.

Cited Studies:

1. Voith VL, Trevejo R, Dowling-Guyer S, Chadik C, Marder A, Johnson V, Irizarry K. Comparison of visual and DNA breed identification of dogs and inter-observer reliability. *American Journal of Sociological Research* 2013; 3:17-29.

2. Hoffman CL, Harrison N, Wolff L, Westgarth C. Is that dog a Pit Bull? A cross-country comparison of perceptions of shelter works regarding breed identification. *Journal of Applied Animal Welfare Science* 2014; 17:322-339.

3. Olson KR, Levy JK, Borby B, Crandall MM, Broadhurst JE, Jacks S, Barton RC, Zimmerman MS. Inconsistent identification of pit bull-type dogs by shelter staff. *The Veterinary Journal* 2015; 206:197-202.

4. Gunter LM, Barber RT, Wynne CDL. What's in a name? Effect of breed perceptions & labeling on attractiveness, adoptions & length of stay for pit-bull-type dogs. *PLoS ONE* 2016; 11: e0146857.doi:10.1371/journal.pone.0146857.

30
Excitable You

The dangers of committing the Fundamental Attribution Error with our dogs.

There is a common cognitive bias, the *Fundamental Attribution Error,* which is central to the way in which we view others and make judgements about their behavior. It is supported by a large body of research and is one of the most common errors that our brains make on a regular basis. The Fundamental Attribution Error refers to our tendency to explain the behavior of other people in terms of their internal disposition, such as personality traits, innate abilities, and motives, rather than to the external (situational) factors that may actually be exerting a much stronger influence on them. This lapse in judgement occurs (especially in Western cultures) because we tend to assign high value to what we assume to be an individual's character and personality traits, while at the same time we underestimate the influence that situational factors and context can have.

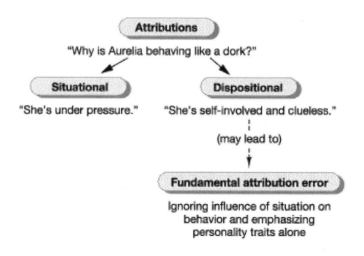

The Fundamental Attribution Error

189

We all are susceptible to committing this error and it is usually only through conscious control that we can keep it in check. A common example occurs when we are driving and someone cuts us off in traffic. We immediately label the offending driver as "a jerk" (or worse) rather than consider that he might be driving to the hospital (or with his dog to the veterinarian) on an emergency and would not normally behave so rudely towards other drivers. This is not to say that unpleasant people do not exist, but rather, that humans have a natural tendency to jump to depositional (personality) explanations for another's behavior and are less inclined to consider situational explanations.

The Fundamental Attribution Error came to mind recently when I was reading a paper that examined dog owners' reports about their dogs' behavior, specifically about excitable behavior. The study was conducted at the Animal Rescue League of Boston and the Center for Shelter Dogs and was published in the journal, *Animals* (1).

The Study: The authors note in the introduction that the term "*excitable behavior*" in dogs is both poorly defined and understudied. They then provide a diverse list of undesirable behaviors that have been reported to fall under the umbrella of *excitable* dog behavior. These include jumping up, mounting, destructiveness, mouthing, grabbing clothing, digging, some forms of barking, rough play, pulling on lead, and (my particular favorite) "*dogs who respond poorly to commands and are difficult to control*". **Study objective:** The purpose of the study was to use an on-line survey to collect information regarding owners' experiences with their dog's excitable behavior and to report the behaviors that are prevalent in excitable dogs. **Methods:** The study group was self-selecting. Participants checked a box in the survey that asked if their dog was "highly excitable or highly energetic". Only those owners who answered "yes" were included in the study; owners who answered "no" were excluded. The remainder of the questionnaire included questions about the dog's demographics and problematic behaviors, and the degree of frustration that the owner had with those behaviors.

Results: The study group included 175 owners, the majority of whom said that they were very frustrated with their dog's behavior and found it difficult to manage. Most of the dogs were spayed/neutered and were young adults (average age; 3 years). Almost half of the dogs (44 %) were identified as either purebred Labrador Retrievers or Lab mixes. The two most frequently reported problematic behaviors were jumping up and mouthing (without discomfort to the person). Other commonly reported undesirable behaviors included general disobedience, unwanted barking, pulling on the leash, destructive behavior and "*not listening to commands*". The scenarios in which excitable behaviors were most likely to occur included when the owner arrived home after an absence and when the owner was playing with the dog. Some owners also reported excessive excitement when the dog was meeting new people.

Conclusions: The authors concluded that "*The majority of owners in this self-selected sample were very frustrated with their excitable dog*", that "*Many of the dogs in the sample had other behavior problems*", and that their results could be used to "*.....provide better education to owners of **excitable dogs**"* (Emphasis mine).

Hmmm........Yes, in case you were wondering, I do have an opinion about this.

I Think I'm Gonna Need a Bigger Box

There are several problems with this study, in terms of both its methodology and with the conclusions that were made. Let's start with that pesky thing called the Scientific Method, which requires the use of both a *representative sample* and *sufficient controls* to prevent bias and capricious conclusions.

Sampling Bias: In the authors' words "*The focus of this study is on owners' experience with their excitable dogs.*" Therefore, it must have seemed logical to them (i.e. it felt like a good idea at the time) to simply ask owners to tell them if their dog was one of those (poorly defined) excitable dogs. By this logic, an excitable dog is a dog who is excitable (according to their owner). Circular reasoning does not a representative sample make. And here's a big surprise; the owners who identified their dog as "highly or extremely excitable" were also very frustrated with their dog's behavior.

Wow. Who knew?

Absence of Controls: At the start of the survey, owners were asked if they would describe their dog as "highly excitable or highly energetic". Only those who answered in the affirmative were included in the study. Owners who answered "no" were not allowed to complete the survey (i.e. a possible control group of dogs was purposefully excluded). The authors went on to report that excitable dogs are likely to show problematic behaviors of jumping up and mouthing, along with a myriad of other associated problem behaviors. However, without a control group to compare the frequencies of these behaviors to, what do we actually learn from these data?

Absolutely Nothing.

Here's Why: Let's say that a control group *was* used (i.e. correct scientific methods were followed). So, hypothetically, let say that the control group included a similar number of age-, sex- and breed-matched dogs who were representative of the general population of dogs. Their owners completed the same survey and answered the same questions. The reported frequencies of problematic behaviors in the experimental group (dogs identified as excitable) were then compared with the frequencies of the same behaviors in the control group. Here are some possible outcomes of this hypothetical study:

- **Jumping up:** In the actual study, 60 percent of owners of excitable dogs said that their dog jumped up to greet when they returned home after an absence. If (hypothetically) a similar proportion of owners in the control group, let's say 62 % for reason of argument, stated that *their* dog jumped on them when they returned home, then the proportion of jumping up in excitable dogs did not differ from the proportion of that problem in the general population of dogs. And, if jumping up was **not** over-represented in the excitable dog group, then jumping up is NOT a problem associated with excitable dogs. (Rather, it is just something that dogs do).

- **Pulling on leash, destructive behaviors, *not listening to commands:*** You see where this is going. The plethora of unwanted dog behaviors that the study participants vented about in their surveys cannot viewed as indicative of an excitable dog because the frequencies of these behaviors were never compared to their frequencies in other dogs.

- This problem is exacerbated by the fact that the owners placed their dogs into the self-described category of excitable dog in the first place. Lots of dogs pull on lead, bark and do not listen. All that we learned here is that owners like to complain about these behaviors and welcome the opportunity to label their dog as "excitable".

Wait, there's more.

The Fundamental Attribution Error: The authors state: "*In general, disobedient, destructive, chasing and barking behavior problems were the most commonly reported behaviors by owners of excitable dogs*". Excluding the occasional dog who cheats on his income taxes or robs the town bank, I think that this list of unwanted behaviors pretty much covers everything that owners complain about in young, untrained dogs. (What are the "non-excitable dogs' doing to annoy their owners, one might ask)?

While this sounds facetious, I actually am serious. If the purpose of this study was to allow a group of self-identifying owners of excitable dogs to air their (numerous) complaints about their dogs and to give their perceptions a voice, then by definition, the authors are assuming that excitable dogs *differ* in some fundamental way from other dogs. I would argue that they have no evidence of such a thing and moreover that classifying certain dogs as *excitable* is ill-founded and not in the best interest of any dogs, regardless of the researchers' noble intentions.

Encouraging dog owners (and dog professionals) to commit a fundamental attribution error by labeling dogs as inherently "excitable" provides tacit permission to blame the dog's personality or intrinsic nature for undesirable behaviors, rather than looking carefully at situational factors that may be influencing the dog.

The outcome of such perceptual differences could be devastating:

Fundamental Attribution Explanations (The Excitable Dog):

- My dog must have been born this way. (*Solution: none*)
- He was abused/abandoned/neglected by his previous owner and it made him hyperactive. (*Solution: none*)
- He's a Lab, Lab-mix, Pittie (*Insert any breed stereotype here) (*Solution: none*)
- She's a hyper-active dog. (*Solution: none*)
- He's an excitable dog. (*Solution: none*)
- ***She's a bad dog. (Solution: Get rid of the dog).***

This mindset leads an owner to the conclusion that their dog's behavior is immutable and that their own degree of responsibility is minimal or nonexistent. Alternatively, where do situational explanations lead us?

Situational Explanations (Unwanted Excited Behaviors):

- He is rarely exposed to new people, places, and dogs. (*Solution: I need to socialize him and take him with me more often*).
- She does not receive regular exercise. (*Solution: I need to incorporate several types of daily exercise into our routines*).
- He has not had consistent training (*Solution: I will enroll him in a training class*).
- She is crated and left alone for many hours of the day. (*Solution: I will hire a dog-walker or use a reputable doggy day care*).
- I may have unrealistic expectations for my young dog's behavior. (*Solution: I will ratchet down my expectations so that they are more in line with what is reasonable to expect of a young, happy and exuberant dog. I will love my dog*).

Let's avoid making the fundamental attribution error with our dogs. Because we have complete control over what happens to them, the outcome can be much worse than simply calling someone a jerk.

Nuff said. Off box.

Cited Study: Shabelansky A, Dowling-Guyer S. Characteristics of excitable dog behavior based on owners' report from a self-selected study. *Animals* 2016; 6, 22; doi10.3390/ani6030022.

31
The Perfect Dog

What are the attributes of your perfect dog? (You may want to be careful about how you reply).

Well, not *perfect* actually, the word that is being thrown around is *ideal*. In three separate studies, people in the UK, Australia and Italy were polled and asked to describe what they believe to be their *ideal* dog; the dog with whom they would like to share their love and their life.

The first survey, conducted in the UK, was not scientific, but rather an informal poll conducted by a popular Sunday paper. "The Express" asked 2000 dog owners about what they considered to be the most desirable physical characteristics in a dog. After collecting the surveys, the editors combined the most popular answers to create a chimera of breed types - medium size with the coat of an English bulldog, the ears of a King Charles spaniel and the happy, wagging tail of an Irish Setter. Other attributes were borrowed from Border Collies, Labrador Retrievers, and Beagles. They even specified the type of bark that the perfect pooch should have - must be "mid-range, not high-pitched". (I guess that rules out Tollers).

Admittedly, this mythical dog was pretty darn cute. However, the newspaper survey did not ask about behavior or temperament, which are really the most important features to think about in one's ideal canine companion. Lucky for us, researchers in Australia and Italy asked exactly these questions (1, 2).

What Australians Like: A group of almost 900 Australian citizens were surveyed regarding both the physical and the behavioral characteristics of their perceived ideal dog, using an on-line survey tool. The majority of respondents were current dog owners (72.3 %) and female (79.8 %). The researchers used a statistical technique called principal component analysis (PCA) to identify consistent clusters of responses among available answers.

Results: The ideal dog for Australians, as measured by this survey, is medium-sized, short-haired, and "de-sexed" (i.e. neutered/spayed). Behaviorally, he is house-trained, friendly, good with children, obedient and healthy. Also of importance were reliably responding to "come" (and its corollary, not running away), and showing affection to one's owner. Oh yeah, and a majority of the respondents said that their perfect dog was *not* a poop eater.

Italians are Going For: One of the researchers in the Australian study (PC Bennett) went on to collaborate with scientists in Italy and administered the same survey to a group of 770 Italian citizens.

Results: Participant demographics were similar to those of the Australian study and behavior traits of the perceived ideal dog were almost identical. The Italian perfect pooch is house-trained, safe with children, friendly, obedient, healthy, and long-lived. There were a few differences between men and women in the two studies, however.

The Gender Gaps: Australian women valued dogs who are calm, obedient, sociable and non-aggressive, while men in that culture went for dogs who are more energetic, protective and faithful. Italian men were significantly more likely than women to prefer an intact (non-neutered) dog, and Italian women were willing to spend more time with their dog than were men.

Conclusions: The researchers placed emphasis on the fact that most dogs who live as companions today are of breeds or breed-types that were originally developed for a specific purpose and work, such as herding, hunting or protecting. However, very few dogs continue to be used for those functions which may contribute to a disconnect between what people perceive the *ideal* dog to be and the reality of how dogs behave and respond to modern-day lifestyles. The results of both studies reported that participants valued a dog's behavior and health more than they do physical appearance. However, the specific behaviors that were strongly valued suggested unrealistic expectations regarding a dog's needs, behavior and training.

The study's authors make two recommendations regarding how this information should be used:

1. ***Education***: The study results show that the general public continues to require education regarding normal and expected behavior of dogs, along with dogs' needs for training. This education can help to reduce the obvious gap that exists between what is perceived to be an ideal dog and real dogs living as companions.

2. ***Selective breeding:*** Because dogs live primarily as companions in homes today, the authors state that breeders should be focusing their efforts on producing dogs that meet owner expectations regarding behavior as opposed to breeding for physical appearance.

My opinion on this research and on the authors' recommendations? Yeah, I got one. Big surprise, I know.

Up on the Ol' Box

The fact that people identified their ideal dog to be one who is house-trained, friendly, obedient and good with kids should hardly come as a surprise. The last time I checked, there are not many people who are seeking a house-soiling, anti-social, diso-bedient baby killer as their next canine companion. I think we can all agree that most people (probably not just Australians and Italians) value, at least to some degree, the traits that these stud-ies reported.

Where things get a little weird (for me) is in the disconnect be-tween what people identified as their ideal dog and the degree to which (if at all) they perceived their own responsibility in trying to achieve that ideal. For example, in both studies, the majority of respondents stated that their ideal dog was acquired as a puppy. Okey Dokey then - Do the math. How exactly does house-trained, coming when called, not running away, good with chil-dren, friendly and healthy come about if not through consistent training, exercise, socialization, veterinary visits and care, *on the part of the owner?*

There was additional evidence that the participants were not thinking this all the way through:

- In the Australian study, although the majority of participants stated that their ideal dog was "obedient", when they were asked about the trainability of this dog *only 3.6 % (or virtual-ly no one)* stated that this was important and approximately one-third believed that "*some dogs cannot be trained*". So, I guess the obedient dog who comes when called, does not run

200

away, and oh yeah, abstains from poop-eating just popped out of the womb like that.

- While the Italian respondents did not share the Australians' views regarding trainability, they made up for it when asked about exercise and grooming needs. Owners who reported that they spent little time exercising and grooming their *actual* dog reported much higher frequencies of these activities with their *ideal dog*. (Perhaps he is more active and has a denser coat?). About 1 in 10 Italians stated that they never walk their dog at all and slightly less reported that they never groomed their (actual) dog.

Who's Responsible? These discrepancies between ideal and actual dogs prompted the researchers to make their two recommendations, listed above. I wholeheartedly agree with Number 1. Number 2? Not so much. In fact, I would argue that the two recommendations are at odds with each other. Here is what I mean:

- **Change expectations:** If one agrees that the studies' results reflect unrealistic expectations by owners about dogs and that these need to be corrected via education (and perhaps the occasional slap upside the head), *it is illogical to follow this by suggesting that breeders attempt to create dogs who meet these unrealistic expectations.*

- **Change breeding focus:** Certainly breeders should be selecting for stable and appropriate temperaments within the standard of their breed. And, I think most would agree that certain breeds (or breed-types) are better suited for families with children or elderly couples or an urban-dwelling professional than others. However, this recommendation appears to suggest that breeders *stop* selecting for behavior traits that tilt away from the (mythical) ideal dog. For example, should Border Collie breeders stop selecting for herding instinct so that little Johnny's heels don't get nipped at as he races around the living room? Should Golden Retriever breeders stop selecting for active dogs so that their owners have no obligation to take the dog for walks? Must Beagle breeders stop breeding sniff-focused dogs because we all know that excessive *sniffiness* promotes wandering off? And, perhaps breeders of long--haired dogs with double coats should cut that nonsense out right now and begin selecting for bald dogs who require no grooming (because picking up that brush a few times a week is just too much work for the busy dog owner).

Sarcasm aside, I would argue that not only are "unrealistic expectations" a problem here, but the term "*ideal*" itself also needs to go. Just as the ideal man does not exist (yes, sad I know, but true), neither does the ideal dog. Border Collies herd, Golden Retrievers chase things and bring them back, hairy dogs shed (and need to be brushed), some dogs are aloof with strangers, some dogs don't like kids all that much, some bark a lot, and yes, Virginia, some dogs like to eat poop. Rather than catering to people's unrealistic beliefs about some mythical dog, let's instead focus on promoting caring for, respecting, and loving the dogs that we have, non-ideal traits and all.

Cited Studies:

1. King T, Marston LC, Bennett PC. Describing the ideal Australian companion dog. *Applied Animal Behaviour Science* 2009; 120:84-93.

2. Diverio S, Boccini B, Menchetti L, Bennett PC. The Italian perception of the "ideal companion dog". *Journal of Veterinary Behavior* 2016; 12:27-35.

32
Go Ask Alice

Perhaps there is no "perfect dog" (nor should there be),
but really now, are not all puppies just naturally perfect?
Why do we love puppies so much?

Last summer, we brought home the newest member of our canine family, Alice. She was 8-weeks-old and cute. Really cute.

This is Ally (When she was just Small)

Not only did we think so. Apparently others did too. Throughout the summer, we could not go walking at our local park without being waylaid by other visitors who would swoop in (often without asking [*sigh*]) to meet the little puppy, hug the little puppy, and play with the little puppy. These interactions were replete with the high-pitched squeaky voice, nonsense words, and scrunched up kissy face that we all know (and sorta don't love). Ally absorbed all of this attention like the little canine diva she is (though, she said that sometimes she would rather go chasing rabbits).

During these interludes, our three adult boys, Cooper, Chippy and Vinny, sat quietly, offering their sit-stays, and hoping to catch a bit of the affection fall-out. However, while handsome, friendly, and oh-so-smart, their obvious adult status just did not pull the same emotional heartstrings as did Ally's little puppy face.

Please share a bit of that lovin' with us.

Go ask Alice: So, I asked Alice if she knew *why* people on the trail would swoon over her whilst ignoring her equally wonderful brothers. I thought she would know. She said without hesitation that it is because of her unbearable puppy cuteness (she added that all of the attention did tend to make her feel 10 feet tall).

Puppy narcissism aside, she was quite right. Research tells us so.

We Like *Baby* Animals: Konrad Lorenz first explained this phenomenon using a concept that he termed "*Kindchenschema*". This refers to a set of universal physical attributes of baby mammals that trigger unconscious affiliative (loving) and caretaking responses in adults. These features include large eyes, a proportionately large and domed skull, shortened limbs and overall "pudgy features". Following Lorenz, the theory that adult humans are naturally drawn to baby mammals has been studied in multiple variants, including with our favorite animal companion, the dog. For example, there is evidence that the infantilism that we see in toy breeds and in dogs with a brachycephalic (smushed nose) facial structure naturally mimic the appearance of puppies and so are highly attractive to many people (1, 2). Other baby animal features that we see in some dogs such as floppy ears, pudgy bodies (natural or *ahem*, acquired), and short legs may be at work creating a canine *Kindchenschema* as well.

However, despite what Alice thinks, we know that our attraction to dogs is not all about puppies. People are also drawn to adult dogs for a variety of reasons. Two recent research studies have identified a few additional canine attributes that seem to attract us.

We Pay Attention to Color and Ears: A study published in 2008 reported that, similar to our tendencies with other people, humans readily assign personality traits to dogs based simply on their appearance (3). However, the study did not attempt to identify specific traits that might influence these perceptions. Recently, Jamie Fratkin and Suzanne Baker at James Madison University in Texas attempted to tease out some of these traits (4). They selected two obvious features that differ among dogs; coat color (yellow vs. black) and ear type (floppy vs. prick). They manipulated the photographs of two dogs to show a black or yellow coat color on one dog and floppy or prick (pointy) ears in the second dog. Study participants completed a questionnaire that rated each dog in terms of the Big Five (human) personality traits; openness, conscientiousness, extraversion, agreeableness and emotional stability.

Results: Both the color of a dog's coat and the set of a dog's ears influenced perceptions of personality. Participants perceived dogs with a yellow coat or floppy ears to be more agreeable and emotionally stable when compared to dogs with a black coat or prick ears, respectively. In addition, a dog with a yellow coat was rated higher in conscientiousness than a dog with a black coat and a dog with prick ears was rated as more extraverted than a dog with floppy ears. (*Note:* The questions that were used to score conscientiousness reflect dependability and self-discipline, which could be interpreted as signifying a dog who is well-behaved and obedient). At its most basic, this set of results tell us that perceptions of a dog's personality are influenced by coat color and ear type in the absence of other information. More specifically, there is a tendency to perceive yellow dogs who have floppy ears more favorably than black dogs with pointy ears.

It Really is (Mostly) About Us: Julie Hecht and Alexandra Horowitz at City University and Barnard College in New York expanded upon this theme and examined the potential influence that a wide range of physical features in dogs may have upon human perceptions (5). They altered 15 different physical features in each of a series of photographs of 28 adult, mix-breed dogs. Each altered photo was then paired with its original. The targeted features fell into one of four categories: juvenile traits (increased size or spacing of eyes and size of the head), human-like traits (presence of a smile, colored irises), size/symmetry attributes, and a single feature related to domestication (piebald coloring). The changes that they made were subtle enough that people were generally unaware of the difference between the two photographs. Study participants were presented with 80 paired images and were asked to simply select which dog they "*liked the best*".

Results: The physical traits that most strongly influenced "*liking*" preferences were the presence of a smile (open mouth, relaxed and retracted commissures) and having colored eye irises. Both of these features occur in human faces and are associated with positive (friendly) emotions. In other words, we tilt towards features that dogs and humans share and that mean similar things. Several, but not all, infantile traits also enhanced a dog's attractiveness. These included having large eyes, increased spacing between the eyes, and smaller jowls. Conversely, the study found no influencing effects of any other facial features, nor for a dog's size, symmetry, or presence of piebald coloring.

Take Away for Dog Folks: Taken together, these studies suggest that dog features that naturally attract us include the infantile (puppy) traits of large eyes, domed skulls and floppy ears, as well as yellow coats (when compared with black). Oh yeah, and we are also attracted to dogs who look similar to friendly people - they smile a lot and their eyes appear friendly and warm.

Why is This Information Important? Despite often knowing (or at least being informed of) the much greater importance of a dog's personality and behavior as the criterion for selecting a pet, many people continue to choose a dog based upon physical appearance. (Ask any experienced shelter worker if you doubt this). People like what they like, and will choose accordingly. And, given the ubiquitous use of web sites and internet services to promote dog adoptions, the first thing that most people see of a dog or puppy who they are considering adopting is *a photograph*.

These studies provide evidence that regardless of trying to convince adopters of the importance of meeting a dog in person, these photographs are an important influencer of adopters' perceptions (correct or not) of canine personality. Thus shelters, rescue groups, and breeders can use this information not only when determining how to best photograph and present a dog on their websites, but also as they educate potential adopters regarding how a dog's appearance may be subconsciously influencing them.

As for Alice, she says that white knights and red queens got nothin' on her being a yellow dog with floppy ears and dark eyes. Seems she is set for life.

Cited Studies:

1. Waller BM, Peirce K, Caeiro C, Scheider L, Burrows AM, McCune S, Kaminski J. Paedomorphic facial expressions give dogs a selective advantage. 2013; *PLoS ONE* 8(12):e826986.doi:10.1371/journal.pone.0092686.

2. Golle J, Lisibach S, Mast FW, Lobmaier JS. Sweet puppies and cute babies: Perceptual adaptation to babyfacedness transfers across species. *PLoS ONE* 2013;8(3):e58248. doi:10:1371/journal.pone.0058248.

3. Kwan VSY, Gosling SD, John OP. Anthropomorphism as a special case of social perception: A cross-species social relations model analysis of humans and dogs. *Social Cognition* 2008; 26:129-142.

4. Fratkin JL, Baker SC. The role of coat color and ear shape on the perception of personality in dogs. *Anthrozoos* 2013; 26:125-133.

5. Hecht J, Horowitz A. Seeing dogs: Human preferences for dog physical attributes. *Anthrozoos* 2015; 28:153-163.

P.S. How many of the references to Alice's namesake song ("*White Rabbit*") did you catch? (Answer: There are nine).

About the Author

Linda Case is a dog trainer, canine nutritionist, and science writer. She earned her B.S. in Animal Science at Cornell University and her M.S. in Canine/Feline Nutrition at the University of Illinois. Following graduate school, Linda was a lecturer in canine and feline science in the Animal Sciences Department at the University of Illinois for 15 years and then taught companion animal behavior and training at the College of Veterinary Medicine.

Linda owns AutumnGold Consulting and Dog Training Center in Mahomet, IL (www.autumngoldconsulting.com), a company that provides scientific writing and training programs to dog owners, pet food companies and animal advocacy organizations. Linda is the author of numerous publications and seven other books, including most recently, *Beware the Straw Man: The Science Dog Explores Dog Training Fact & Fiction* (AutumnGold Publishing, 2015) and *Dog Food Logic: Making Smart Decisions for your Dog in an Age of Too Many Choices* (Dogwise, 2014). She also authors the popular blog "*The Science Dog*" which regularly reviews new research in canine behavior, training, nutrition and health and where many of the essays in "*Only Have Eyes for You*" originated (http://thesciencedog.wordpress.com).

Linda and her husband Mike share their lives with four dogs; Vinny, Chip, Cooper and Alice, and Pete the cat. In addition to dog training, Linda enjoys running, hiking, swimming, and gardening— all activities that she happily shares with her dogs.

Contact information:
Linda P. Case, MS
Owner, AutumnGold Consulting and Dog Training Center
www.autumngoldconsulting.com

Made in the USA
San Bernardino, CA
31 March 2018